INSIDE
THE GREAT
TANKS

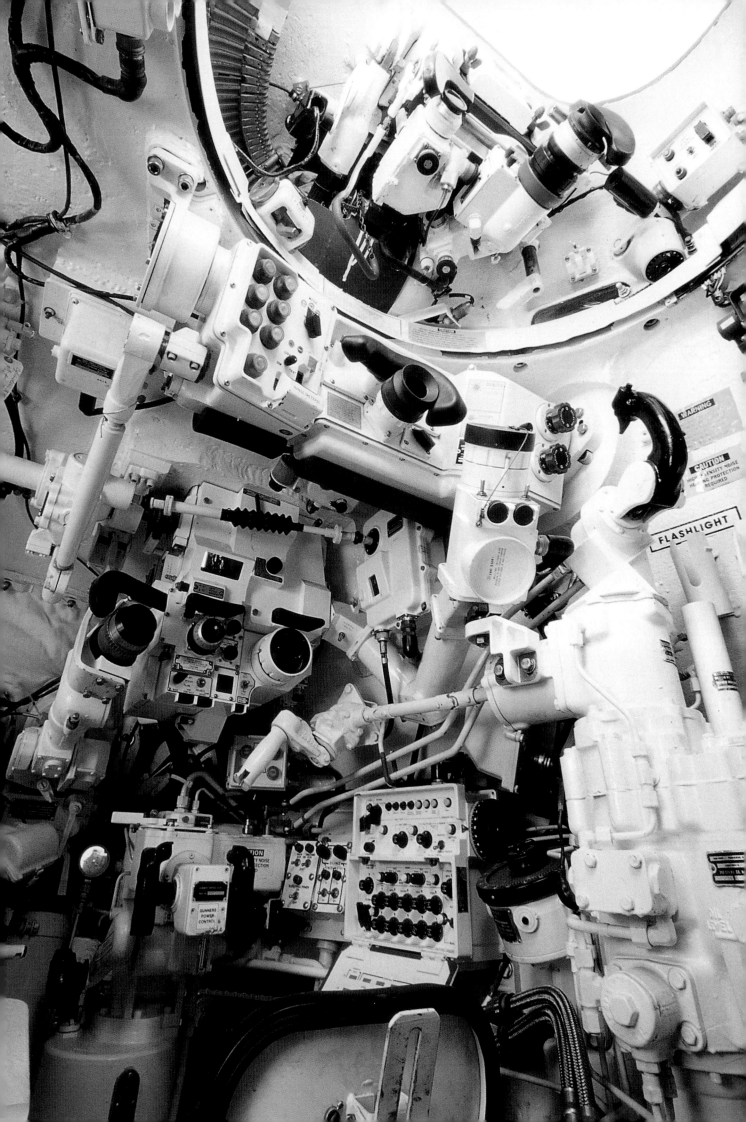

INSIDE THE GREAT TANKS

Hans Halberstadt

THE CROWOOD PRESS

This edition published in
Great Britain 1998 by
The Crowood Press Ltd
Ramsbury, Marlborough
Wiltshire SN8 2HR

This impression 2000
Printed by Leo Paper Products, China
Designed by Tony Stocks/TS Graphics

A CIP catalogue record for this book
is available from the British Library

ISBN 1 86126 270 1

Stock photography
All photographs in this book (and about
60,000 other military photos) are available
as stock images for editorial and advertising
applications. Direct inquiries to:
Tanks A Lot
240 South 13th Street
San Jose, California USA 95112
telephone: (408) 293-8131
fax: (408) 293-8156

Dedication
For Jacques Littlefield, with a salute and thanks.

Acknowledgements

I am grateful for help in the completion of this book to
several folks who know a lot more about armor than I do:
Jacques Littlefield for one, and Mike Green for another.
Jacques has made a life-long study of armor technology and
evolution, and Mike has very generously shared his extensive
library and armor experience with me. I am also indebted
to Keith Boles, Roy Hamilton and Greg Taylor for helping
move and position the vehicles for photography. I am likewise grateful for the insights of the folks who have actually
operated these tanks and shared the experience with us all:
Marc Sehring, Dean and Nancy Klefman, Richard Boyd,
Duane Klug, and Charles Lemons of the Patton Tank
Museum at Fort Knox, Kentucky. We also wish to acknowl-
edge our debt to the published standard reference works of
such well-known armor experts as Maj. James Bingham,
Simon Dunstan, Jim Mesko, Brian Perrett, Bart Vanderveen
and Steven J. Zaloga.

Special thanks are also due to several World War II combat
veterans: to the legendary Col. James Leach, USA (Ret.),
Col. William Marshall, USA (Ret.), and John Whitehill.
Anybody interested in armor is advised to visit the premiere
collection of historic tanks in the USA - the Patton Museum
at Fort Knox, Kentucky; while many US Army installations
have museums open to the public, the Patton Museum is
probably the best dedicated to tanks and armored vehicles.
The equivalent in the United Kingdom is the Tank Museum
at Bovington Camp, Wareham, Dorset.

Preface

In the broad spectrum of books about armor, this is an
unusual one: it takes the reader inside some of the most
important, battle-proven armored fighting vehicles from
World War II to the present day. There are lots of books
about tanks, but not many that show you what lurks inside
that thick armored hide, where all the action actually
occurs; and those featuring the M1 Abrams are among the
first ever made inside the turret, and required special
dispensation from the US Army. But the really remarkable
thing about this book is that these handsome vehicles are -
except for the M60A3 and M1 Abrams - to be found in the
private collection of Jacques Littlefield. He and his crew
have acquired, restored, and maintained one of the best
collections of armor in the world, and Jacques has been kind
enough to share them with students of armor through this
publication.

An explanation is perhaps due at the outset: while the
tanks featured in this book are certainly "great", we cannot
pretend to include all the "great tanks". Notable ommis-
sions are the classic German Panzers from World War II, of
which the very few existing examples in private hands are
not yet restored and accessible. While the Littlefield collection does include some interesting British types of World
War II and later - the Churchill, Comet, Valentine, and
Centurion - these are not yet restored to a suitable standard
for photography in this book. Depending upon the reception
this book achieves, we may perhaps attempt a further
volume in a year or two.

Hans Halberstadt
San Jose, California

CONTENTS

Chapter 1
Warning Order

Just before midnight - about an hour after he had finally bedded down by his tank - a call on the radio summoned the company commander up to the Tactical Operations Center (TOC) to receive his operation order. He collected his web gear, weapon, helmet and map case, and staggered off into the night.

He was back an hour later, rousing and calling together the platoon leaders and platoon sergeants, the executive officer and first sergeant to hear the "op order". This one, like many before it, was a "movement to contact" against an enemy force 20 "klicks" down the road and over the next ridge. The platoons had received their warning order early the previous evening; expecting to kick off at 0400 hours, they had planned back from that time, and after doing their prep they had bedded down to get what sleep they could.

Just three klicks back down the road at the assembly area the four tanks of each platoon were ready: fuel tanks topped off, main gun racks and machine gun ammunition bins replenished by the battalion support platoon. The sixteen men (including one boyish lieutenant) had already been fighting for three weeks now, and knew the drill. Nobody had to talk much, and nobody did.

The tank commanders (TCs) woke their crews at 0300 hours - those who had been able to sleep - and prepared for battle. Bedrolls and camouflage nets were secured in the bustle rack, "meals ready to eat" (MREs) were distributed, and coffee was brewed in canteen cups on tiny backpackers' stoves. Then the crews clambered up and disappeared into their vehicles, wriggling down into their stations, waiting and watching for the curtain to rise. Off in the distance beyond the ridge artillery muttered, the flashes from the tubes flickering from the clouds floating over the battlefield.

At 0355 each driver reached for the master switch that energizes the electrical system of his tank, switching it to ON. Each driver worked through the engine pre-start checklist, just as he had done so many times before. At exactly 0400 the START switch for each of the four engines in the platoon, the 17 engines in the company, and the 58 tanks in the battalion rumbled into life. One by one, the platoons made a brief radio check; then the leader of each platoon reported to the company commander: "Up!"

"Driver, move out", orders the TC. On the command, in sequence, each tank moves out on to the road, into the night. If you've never stood in the hatch of a tank in the hours before dawn and before a certain fight, here's something of what it

feels like: you seem to float above the ground, the hull of the tank pivoting gracefully and ponderously beneath your feet. Despite its huge bulk and massive weight a tank often seems to glide across the landscape, floating smoothly.

The long column of combat vehicles - tanks in the lead, followed by the infantry in personnel carriers, the command tracks, the logistics train with its fuel, food, spare parts - thunders down out of the valley into more open ground, eating up the kilometers between the friendly force and the enemy.

About seven klicks short of the known enemy positions the lead element of the attack shifts from a column formation - one tank following the next - into its combat formation, according to the unit's SOP. Each platoon reports to the commander as they cross the "line of departure", the place on the map where the attack begins: "Second Platoon, Bravo, LD". The commander, listening on the battalion net, has his ducks in a row.

Each four-tank platoon spreads out into a shallow wedge formation, with the platoon commander centre right, the platoon sergeant centre left, and the two "wingmen" on the outside. Each tank has a designated field of fire, and the TCs and gunners search intently for enemy targets and threats as, roaring across the landscape at better than 20 miles per hour, the force begins to sweep down on the defenders.

The defending enemy have only been in their positions overnight, and their engineer force has worked furiously to obstruct just such an attack, observed by friendly scouts. Tank ditches, minefields, barbed wire, anti-tank teams, and dug-in tanks with just their turrets visible are all waiting for the inevitable attack. A tank attack can't be avoided, but it can be channelled into killing zones where the attackers can be ground down until their force is spent. But one night is not much time: no defense is ever perfect or complete, as the enemy commander knows full well. The friendly task force commander knows where some of the obstacles are, thanks to the scouts and to observation aircraft.

First light finds an armored brigade descending on a defending regiment, the force closing at a relentless rate of 20 kilometers an hour. The defenders, and the objective, are enveloped in dust, smoke, and fire from the artillery and air prep fires. Attack helicopters roar past the lead elements, flit across the terrain from one hiding place to another, and attack survivors in the enemy position, their anti-tank missiles streaking into the objective like horizontal lighting. The flashes of warhead impacts are followed by secondary explosions as tanks come suddenly unzipped in massive fireballs. Streams of tracers float out from some of the attack helicopters, a hail of 20mm and 30mm cannon fire that chews up the enemy's thin-skinned support vehicles and infantry.

Out of the gloom, the attacking tankers can see muzzle flashes from the defenders. One attack helicopter pops up to launch a missile; an enemy tank, unnoticed in the melee, takes him out with a shot from the main gun, the sabot projectile streaking across the battlefield at over a mile per second; its tracer forms a straight, deadly line from tank to helicopter, punctuated by a ball of fire and falling metal.

Five klicks from the forward line of enemy tanks the first artillery rounds start to fall on the force. Four klicks from the enemy, the first tank rounds are fired - ineffectually, as it happens, and revealing the positions of the enemy. Inside the attacking tanks commanders and gunners scan for targets. You can't see very well through the vision blocks, but you can't get killed by a sniper's bullet or shell fragment from inside the turret, either. As the lead elements of the assault come into range, the radio comes alive with spot reports from the tanks as they begin to identify and fire on the enemy:

"Sabre Six, this is Red One - spot report", calls one of the tanks to the company commander, offering information.

"Roger, Red One, send it," the CO answers.

"Roger Sabre Six; observed recon vehicle vicinity Papa Alpha six seven four eight three - disappeared before I could engage, moving southwest."

One TC spots an enemy tank scuttling out of the way of the advance, and makes a hasty call to the CO: "Red Six, engaging two T-72s vicinity of house on woodline, now, out!"
He grasps his pistolgrip control for the main gun, depressing a switch on the side; the loud whine of the turret motor hydraulics is added to the roar inside the tank, and a control circuit snatches authority for the gun away from the gunner sitting just forward of the TC's legs.

The TC rotates his grip left, and the turret and gun slew rapidly round. "GUNNER!", he calls; "SABOT! TANK! AT MY COMMAND!"

The TC swings the gun toward the enemy tank, which is still moving, over a mile away. The enemy vehicle appears in the gunner's sight, and when he sees the target materialize in his field of view he answers, "IDENTIFIED!" The TC releases his grip on his over-ride control, allowing the gunner to take over the engagement; and the gunner lays the reticle onto the center of mass of the target. The loader, on the left side of the turret across the gun breech from the TC, selects a sabot round from the ready ammunition rack and heaves it into the gaping breech of the main gun; the breech slams closed three seconds after the command. The loader rams the safety control from SAFE to FIRE, and calls "UP!".

"FIRE!", calls the commander. "ON THE WAY!", responds the gunner as he presses the firing trigger, launching the round downrange. The sound of the huge main gun firing isn't especially loud from inside the buttoned-up turret, but the gun recoils fiercely as it launches its projectile at a mile per second. The TC and gunner both watch the round streak across the battlefield, the red tracer element marking its brief, bright journey. A momentary cloud of dust and fire obscures the round, but quickly clears to reveal the tracer streaking toward the center of mass of the distant tank.

The projectile - a 15 pound needle made from depleted uranium, only about an inch-and-a-half in diameter and 15 inches long - strikes the side of the enemy tank's turret at a velocity of about 4,500 feet per second. In a couple of microseconds the kinetic energy of this heavy, slender arrow melts right through the heavy armor and sprays molten steel throughout the interior of the target tank. Several main gun rounds in the target's internal racks are struck by the incandescent spray, their propellant detonating catastrophically in the enclosed space. The TC and gunner watch in solemn fascination as the target blossoms in a ball of fire, the huge turret tossed 50 feet into the air like an old skillet....

The platoons, companies, and battalions take their objectives, the enemy survivors routed. Their eyes pressed against their cushioned optics, each crew sweeps the terrain from side to side, searching for surviving threats like missile teams or disabled tanks still able to fire. Tumbling from their armored carriers, the infantry search all the nooks and crannies of the battlefield; unheard from inside the tank turrets their small arms rattle, and grenades detonate with muffled cracks in the enemy trenches and dugouts. They emerge, some herding prisoners before them. The operation is over. The tank platoons fall back to the reverse slope of the objective, take up positions to resist any counterattack, and report.

★   ★   ★

This scenario - with variations, depending upon the current state of the art - has been played out thousands of times since the 1940s. The tanks and tankers on each end of the equation have been American, British, German, Russian, French, North and South Korean, Israeli, Egyptian, Syrian, Jordanian, Indian, Pakistani, Chinese.... Tank warfare today, 80 years after its primitive beginnings, is essentially the same as it was back in September 1939 when German Panzers invaded Poland. The tanks in service today are bigger and faster, shoot farther and more accurately, can see and navigate and communicate with far greater precision and sophistication; but the fundamentals remain unchanged. Those fundamentals are firepower, mobility, and protection, and involve competing compromises.

A big gun and heavy armor inhibit a fighting vehicle's mobility. It is quite possible to provide heavy firepower while still retaining excellent mobility (e.g. the M551 Sheridan); but then the only way to keep the vehicle's weight within practical limits is to sacrifice protection. Likewise, some tanks have had massive firepower and armor (e.g. the legendary German Tiger), but were so ponderous that few bridges could survive their passage. So, traditionally, tank designers have traded off one part of the equation or the other. Only recently, with the advent of the gas turbine-powered M1 Abrams in the 1980s, has a tank combined a high level of all three elements in a single design - although at tremendous financial cost per tank.

Tanks of an Abrams platoon manoeuvre in "combat wedge" formation, each tank covering its partner and each pair of tanks covering the other two. The formation is very like the classic "finger four" used by fighter aircraft.

Portrait of a Tank Crew

The typical crew of most tanks in service today comprises four men: a driver, gunner, loader and commander. Each has a set of very specific responsibilities, and most are cross-trained in at least one other skill.

Loader

The loader is the "entry-level" job for apprentice tankers fresh from Armor School; but it still requires considerable skill, strength, and judgment. In most Western tank crews the loader's position is in the turret to the left of the main gun. His primary job is to serve it, selecting ammunition - typically either "sabot" (see bottom right) or "HEAT" (see top right) rounds - from the ready rack, as directed by the TC or gunner. The sabot round is a slim rod of tungsten carbide or depleted uranium surrounded by an aluminum "shoe" which bulks it out to fit the caliber of the gun; this falls away as the rod leaves the muzzle. Sabot rounds are used against tanks; they contain no explosive, relying on kinetic energy to burn through armor and flake off deadly superheated "spall" inside the target. Sabot rounds fired by the M1 Abrams during Operation Desert Storm not only cut right through Iraqi T-72 tanks from one side to another; on some occasions they went through protective earth berms, then through the tank, then through the berm on the far side.... HEAT (High Explosive Anti Tank) rounds are today used mainly against bunkers, buildings, thin-skinned vehicles, gunpits, and troops in the open.

Except during combat, the loader usually stands in his hatch in the turret roof, manning his externally mounted machine gun and scanning for targets on the left side and rear of the tank. These days it is unrealistic to hope to shoot down attacking aircraft with a hand-held MG; but it is useful for engaging any infantry armed with anti-tank rockets or missiles.

When serving the main gun, the loader waits for a command from the gunner or TC - something along the lines of "Gunner, sabot, tank!". While the gunner is identifying the target the loader stuffs a fresh sabot round into the tube. These days the loader starts the sequence by opening the armored door over the ammunition stowage by hitting a big knee switch, then releasing the round he wants from the ready rack. In the M60 he flips a latch that retains the round, and a spring gives it a push to allow him to get his fingers round its base rim; grasping the base with one hand, he extracts the case and flips it end for end to bring the nose forward, reclosing the doors over the rack by hitting the knee switch again before swivelling round to face the gun. The nose of the projectile is guided into the breech with the left hand, the right hand pushing the base home. The loader seats the round with a closed and gloved fist, knuckles up, to avoid getting his fingers clipped off - the breech block slides upward as soon as the round is fully seated in the chamber. As the breech slams closed, the loader reaches over and hits the safety button; and the gun is ready to fire - in American tanks, he informs the gunner and TC by calling "Up!" when the safety is set to the FIRE position. Armor officer *Richard Boyd*:

"There is a considerable difference between loading a 105mm M60 or M1 round and a 120mm M1A1 round, which is substantially heavier. I've known guys who could 'vacuum-load' a 105 round - run the fresh round up into the breech as the gun recoils from the previous shot - and that takes considerable speed and strength. And I know guys who could load the 105mm round with one hand, gripping the base of the round alone; that also takes considerable strength. But I don't know anybody who could do either with the 120mm round!"

(Above) The loader in an M1 Abrams crew withdraws a 105mm round from the armor-protected ammo stowage in the rear of the turret; the door control is the large pad immediately beyond his right knee.

(Left & opposite) The M1 driver's isolated "armored foxhole" centered in the glacis plate immediately in front of the turret ring. Driving "head up" gives excellent visibility, but exposes him to the weather, flying mud, and enemy fire; with his seat and control handlebars lowered and his hatch "buttoned up" he is dry and protected, but reliant on his periscopes and night vision device.

Driver

Physically separated from the rest of the crew in his compartment at the front, the driver is fully focused on moving the tank across the ground, at the TC's direction.

You scramble up onto the glacis plate, squeeze through your hatch, and slither down into the seat; this can be adjusted up or down, for driving with the hatch open or "buttoned up". The starting sequence for most tanks is pretty simple: there is a master electrical switch, normally on one of the instrument panels; switch it to ON, and the "idiot lights" will illuminate. The fuel shut-off switch is opened. Some tanks require priming, while others don't (except in cold weather). Tanks with radial engines, like the old World War II M4 Sherman, needed hand-cranking of the engine before cold starts (50 turns for the M4A1) to clear the cylinders. Then, in older tanks with reciprocating engines, you typically press the starter and the magneto boost switch; then switch the magneto control to BOTH, and the beast should fire right up. The vastly more modern and sophisticated M1 Abrams, with its gas turbine engine, is even simpler: just press and hold the engine start button, and the process is automatic.

If your tank has been on radio watch all night and working off the batteries, there's a chance you won't have enough juice to get started. Then you must humble yourself in front of your jeering comrades by asking one of the other AFVs in the unit to "slave" or jump-start you, with a heavy cable connecting outlets in the two drivers' compartments.

Former US Army armor officer *Duane Klug*, a volunteer at the Patton Tank Museum at Fort Knox, Kentucky, gets to drive just about anything with tracks on the bottom:

"Tanks can give quite a rough ride - except for the M1, which is wonderful. You've got to pick your route carefully; I never threw a track, but there were times when I came close. You need to apply bursts of power, then back off, sometimes applying the brake as you cross ditches, logs, and uneven terrain. The M60 makes this very easy with just a two-speed

automatic transmission; other tanks, particularly the early ones, can be a bear to shift, particularly when you're coming down. The German World War II Hetzer is an exception - you preselect the gear you want, press the clutch in, then let it out, and you're in that gear. The Sherman is much more difficult and demanding, requiring double-clutching when shifting down. You can get real busy when you're trying to handle two laterals, the accelerator, and the shifting lever all at the same time."

All modern tanks are designed to negotiate ditches up to seven feet across or more, and obstacles about three feet high. In a combat environment the driver's skill has a lot to do with how well the tank gets across, if at all, and whether it throws a track. *Duane Klug* learned to drive an M60 early in his Army career: "I remember crossing ditches seven feet across and about four feet deep. Once you nosed down into one of those things, you were looking at dirt for quite a while, then up at the sky for quite a while coming out the other side."

Richard Boyd, who commanded a tank platoon in the early 1980s, has this to say about the driver's job: "The thing that required a significant amount of training and experience was dealing with obstacles without getting stuck or throwing a track. The M60A3 could go some quite astonishing places - places most people would think were impossible - because of an experienced, capable driver. I've taken one down a 60-percent gradient and done a double dog-leg at the bottom, without throwing a track. You can do that with a well-maintained tank, a tightly tensioned set of tracks, and a good driver.

"Driving a tank in a tactical environment requires several things: the tracks, in particular, need to be in good shape and correctly tensioned. Obstacles need to be approached straight-on wherever possible, rather than at an angle, to avoid throwing a track. A driver needs to learn when and how to brake and accelerate when crossing obstacles. The real problem for the driver is dealing with mud, slopes, craters, snow and ice."

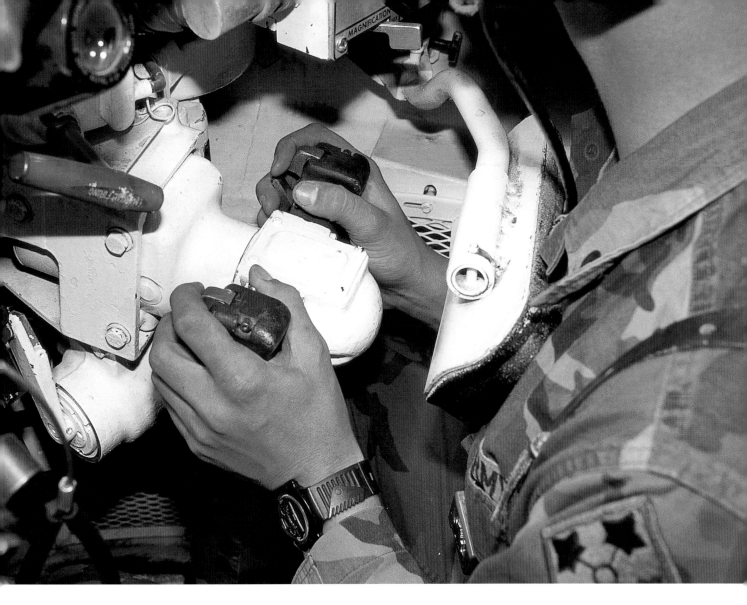

Gunner

The gunner is buried deep inside the tank - in American AFVs, on the right side of the main gun breech; he is the only member of the crew without a hatch of his own, and he depends on getting second helpings of the commander's hatch above and behind him for access, and such daylight and fresh air as he ever sees. Through his optics he constantly scans for targets, traversing the turret back and forth, covering his tank's field of fire.

In modern Western tanks he controls the gun with a pair of power control handles. Far simpler than the old separated elevating wheel and traverse control of World War II tanks, this H-shaped device tilts fore and aft and rotates to the left or right to elevate and traverse the main gun, and also incorporates the activating switches for the laser range-finder and the firing trigger.

In combat, the gunner jams his helmet up against the pad surrounding the eyepiece of his sophisticated sights. If his seat is properly adjusted and the chest rest is correctly positioned, he can lock himself into his sight and can maintain his scan while the tank rocks and rolls across the terrain.

Until the advent of the Muzzle Reference Device (MRD) on the M1 gun tube, gunners had to bore-sight their guns several times a day, correcting for the inevitable drift that occurs in sight systems. The MRD automatically corrects for the natural warping of the gun tube caused by the warmth of the sun on its upper surface. *Richard Boyd* explains part of the gunner's demanding duty:

"The gunner has, in many ways, the most technical job in the tank crew. It takes close attention to detail to hit the right switches in the right sequence at the right time. There is a very high degree of hand-eye co-ordination required. The gunner has to make the same precision G-pattern lay onto the

(Opposite) The M1 gunner's station: wedged into his seat, with pads in front of his helmet and chest, he can concentrate on searching out and engaging targets even while the tank is in motion over rough terrain, without too many black eyes and chipped teeth. **(Above)** The gun control handles - known to US tankers as "Cadillacs", as they are made by Cadillac-Gage - incorporate all the turret traverse, gun elevation, laser range-finder and firing controls. With thorough training they can be manipulated instinctively to track targets nearly two miles away, hand and eye co-ordinating almost as naturally as when a hunter swings his shotgun.

target each time to get consistent hits, and he has to do it very fast. Every tank gun has a little slack or play in its mechanism; to minimize that, you should always bring the gun onto the target the same way you boresight the gun.

"Normally that means bringing the gun across the top of the target from right to left, then down, then below and across from left to right until the tube is directly beneath the target, then upward to its center of mass. (This movement forms a G-shape, hence the name.) The most important part of this is the last vertical movement, because the greatest proportion of error is likely to be either in range or lay."

The gunner will usually have his targets designated by the TC, but in an emergency can engage a threat on his own. The exception to this is when the TC is busy with the .50cal MG mounted near his station, perhaps firing at thin-skinned targets, while heavy armor targets are available within range; then he may release the gunner from his control by making the call, "Gunner - acquire and engage, TC caliber .50!"

Commander

The TC has several simultaneous tasks. As the crew member with the best visibility and communications he maintains "situational awareness" - jargon meaning simply that because he can see better, and talk to other tanks, he should know what's going on at any given moment. He keeps the tank moving toward its objective as part of the tactical plan, co-ordinated with the other tanks in the platoon; that means ensuring that the driver maintains position within the platoon formation. He watches all around the tank, observing terrain and targets; he directs the use of the main gun, but he also has a heavy machine gun of his own. He is typically the only member of the crew who communicates over the radio to other tanks, passing reports and making requests, and - if he's the platoon leader - issuing orders. At night he ensures that the crew maintain and service the tank as required to keep it in fighting condition. Ex-TC *Richard Boyd*:

"The commander spends most of his time isolated from the rest of the crew, with his head up out of the hatch. He doesn't see the other crewmen, he just talks to them. He scans for targets, with binoculars or with the naked eye, and he has to maintain situational awareness at all times - understanding exactly where he is and what's going on outside the tank."

Riding in a tank for any length of time can be fatiguing. There is constant vibration. Modern tank design emphasizes a kind of "sports car" ergonomics for the crew - you don't move around much. That's particularly true for the driver, whose seat gives him a semi-reclining position (in any modern Western tank the driver's position tends to be the most comfortable). Of his days as a platoon and company commander in Germany, *Duane Klug* recalls:

"Especially with the M60 and the Abrams, you get a tremendous feeling of power while moving across the landscape. You learn how to hold on, how to ride the tank, how to anticipate the jolts and the way you get slammed around."

John Whitehill, a veteran of the 4th Armored Division's epic charge across France in 1944, summarizes the relationships within a tank crew: "We were closer together than guys in a submarine - shoulder to shoulder, jammed into that vehicle. We cooked our meals on one little Coleman one-burner stove, in a 'liberated' frying pan from a German field kitchen, and the five of us ate right out of that pan, passing it around and taking turns. That is pretty intimate, and a good example of how close we were. Another thing: we always had a stash of wine and maybe brandy, also liberated from someplace or other, and after a skirmish I'd get out a bottle and pass it around. The five of us would kill that bottle, and as the officer, I waited till last - and sometimes there wasn't too much left in that bottle! A bottle of wine doesn't go too far under those circumstances.

"Something else you don't hear about too often, but important to tank crews, was the problem of relieving yourself - and after a fight, everybody needed to go. Well, it was the loader's responsibility to save the last empty shell casing, and this, too, was passed around inside the turret - again, with the TC or officer getting the last turn - and then the case was tossed over the side. This wasn't the easiest thing to do, since the brass could still be quite hot! If you looked out at the tanks right after a battle, you'd see all these casings flying through the air...."

(Left) An Abrams commander of the 4th Infantry Division scans the surroundings through his cupola vision blocks, his right hand on his gun over-ride control stick. In front of his face are his sights for the .50 cal machine gun (white) and main gun (black pad), and .50 cal elevation control (red).

Col. William Marshall joined the US Army in 1939 when the Cavalry still had horses. After exchanging his mount for an AFV in 1941, in 1944 he came ashore in Normandy on D+30. "The secret of our success", he recalls, "was a carry-over from the Cavalry. In the Cav you worry about your horse and your squad; in the Tank Corps you worry about your tank and your crew. We trained hard together, and we built a going organization, and we were good! We shipped out to England, picked up M4A2 Shermans, and started training. We fired and manoeuvered day and night. And we were fortunate to have a commander - Edgar T. Connely - who was just as intense about the mission as we were. We became the 8th Tank Battalion [4th Armd. Div.], and we went across the beach at Normandy and all the way to the Rhine in 181 days.

"One morning about 0500 I received a mission to attack across the Moiselle River to relieve pressure on the 35th Infantry to our front. I found a spot where it looked like we could ford the river, but the bank on the far side was too steep for us to get over easily. So I sent for my tanks, lined them up hub-to-hub, and we each fired five rounds, fuse-delay. That blew the opposite bank down enough that we had a ramp way out of the water. I went across first, and we all got across. That helped turn the right flank of the German army, and helped relieve some pressure on the British forces to our north. Gen. Patton was in the area about fifteen days later, and awarded me the Distinguished Service Cross for the action.

"When we first broke out of Normandy the German tank units we encountered fired a volley at us, then turned and ran. Most of the hits we got were in the rear of their tanks, and we blew them off the road!

"Here's how combat operations worked for us in France and Germany: we always had scouts out, up forward, and they'd warn us of any enemy forces in our route of march. They might be 500 or 1,000 yards ahead, usually in jeeps or halftracks. The scouts would call us on the radio and we'd shake a leg and get up there. The Germans had tanks that were more powerful than ours, but we fought them successfully because we had a lot of tanks ....Although our gun was smaller than theirs, we closed to under 750 yards and attacked them as a team. We out-manoeuvered them, and then five or six of us would close in on a Panther and we'd all start firing on him, and we'd kill him. The German tanks had better armor, a better gun, better steering; but we destroyed them anyway."

Anatomy of a Tank

The Gun and Turret

The tank's fundamental mission has always been to carry a gun and its crew safely into enemy lines; and it is around the gun that the tank is designed. Tank warfare has always been a race between the designers of better guns and better protection, advantage tilting first one way, then the other.

At the outset of World War II tanks like the British Matilda, US Stuart and their equivalents went into battle with guns firing projectiles of only about 37-40mm diameter, with muzzle velocities of about 2,800 feet per second. Today, the M1A1 Abrams has a 120mm gun which sends vastly more sophisticated projectiles downrange at over 5,000 feet per second. In 1940 the Matilda briefly seemed almost invulnerable with a maximum armor thickness of 78mm; today's Abrams and Challengers have composite "Chobham" armor which probably gives equivalent protection to 400-500mm of steel.

A tank's main gun is expected to engage two kinds of targets: first and foremost, enemy tanks; and secondly, fortifications, emplacements, and other "point" targets. For the past 50 years the gun has typically been designed for extremely flat trajectories, with a very high velocity round. The German 88mm gun, adapted from an anti-aircraft weapon and mounted in the Tiger tank, was the dominant tank gun of 1942-45. The 120mm-plus rounds provided for by today's tank designers streak across the battlefield at a rate of about a mile per second, and are effective against tanks at up to three kilometers range.

The gun is mounted in an armored turret allowing 360-degree rotation and protecting the fighting members of the crew. However big a tank appears from outside, turrets have always been cramped. Ammunition is bulky, and has priority; every technical advance adds more "black boxes" to be mounted around the inside; and under combat conditions every cranny is stuffed with spares for the optics, batteries, rations, canteens, personal kit and weapons, and dozens of other essentials. Since the 1940s tankers have had to stow their bedrolls, packs, water and cooking gear in the exposed baskets on the outside of the turret.

The basic turret structure has normally been of cast steel alloy armor, far thicker on the front than the sides. Historically the roof was surprisingly thin; today sophisticated air-delivered anti-tank munitions have led to increased overhead protection. The main gun is mounted in the turret on a pair of trunnions - the bearing surfaces on which the tube pivots vertically. Since these trunnions and their mounting points absorb the recoil of the weapon they are of massive construction.

The fighting compartment for the crew, rotating with the gun, has normally been a drum-shaped "basket" structure mounted below the turret ring, only partially enclosed so that the crew have access to ammunition and other stowage in various parts of the hull. Electrical continuity between hull and rotating turret is obviously impossible with fixed wiring; tanks have a large rotary connector at the centre of the turret floor, the lower part fixed and the upper allowed to rotate, containing the circuits serving all the turret-mounted components - radios, fire control systems, lighting, etc.

(Opposite) The 105mm gun and turret of an M1 Abrams of the US Army's 4th Infantry Division at Fort Carson, Colorado. The TC (left) and loader (right) man respectively .50cal and 7.62mm externally mounted machine guns. The huge, boxy appearance of the turret is quite deceptive: most of its bulk is taken up by its spaced composite armor, and the internal dimensions are not all that much less cramped than in previous generations of tanks.

(Below) "Say aaah...": an M60 Patton turret in the workshop with gun removed offers an unusual view of the massive cast steel armor and the gun trunnions. Note ammo stowage racks back in the rear bustle of the turret.

(Left) In 1940/41 the Matilda's 40mm (2-pounder) gun was considered - and briefly proved - quite adequate for tank-vs.-tank combat.

(Below) Within the hull shell hundreds of different components and assemblies have to be "wired and plumbed" in; this is an M88 undergoing major overhaul. Note the black-wrapped torsion bars across the floor - these are the essential element of the suspension, each supporting one of the road wheels.

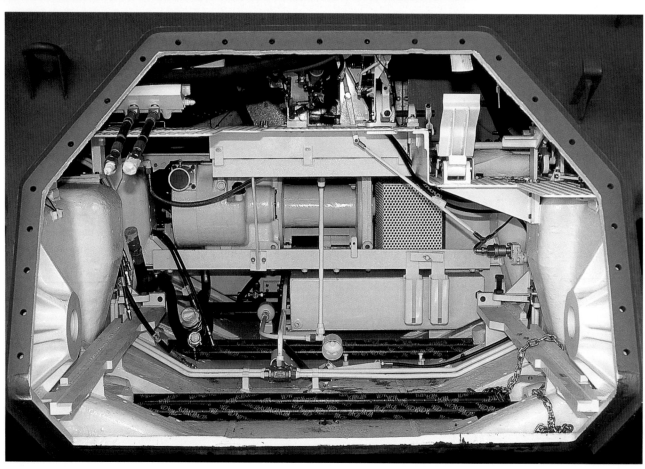

Hull

Tank hulls are typically fabricated from plate armor, although some (like the early M4 Sherman) have used huge cast components. The armor typically comprises over half the weight of the vehicle. Many early World War II tanks used face-hardened steel armor, a difficult material to work; these are generally recognizable by their bolted construction. Cast armor allows for variations in thickness within a single component - typically, thick at the front, theoretically facing the enemy, and thinner at the sides and rear.

Steel armor on the front surfaces of main battle tanks can easily be over four inches (100mm) thick and is sloped, sometimes at a high angle, to deflect impacting projectiles. An angle of 60 degrees effectively doubles the protective value of a given thickness of armor.

The hull is normally intended to be watertight, although few tanks will float; many, however, can wade through rivers and streams up to three or four feet deep without preparation, and can even drive across riverbeds completely submerged if fitted with a snorkel breather system for the engine. (In World War II tanks were sometimes extensively modified in order to "swim" ashore from landing craft or to make submerged crossings.)

In nearly all tanks the driving compartment is positioned in the front of the hull; the engine at the rear, behind a solid bulkhead; and the turret, with its suspended fighting compartment, amidships. The turret mounting ring and the surrounding area of the hull are centrally important elements of tank design; they must absorb the full force of the main gun recoil. Battle damage to the ring of bearings on which the turret rides can easily jam it, leaving the tank more or less helpless; the turret ring has always been a classic aiming point for enemy gunners.

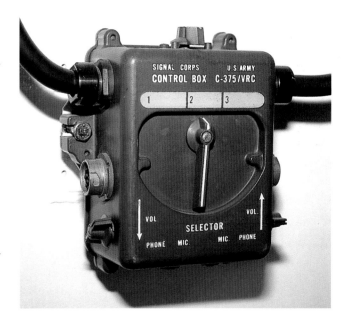

(Above) Internal assemblies are usually simply mounted to the "raw" inside surfaces of tank turrets and hulls; this is a communications switch box.

(Below) The engine has been lifted out of its rear hull compartment during overhaul of this M41 tank.

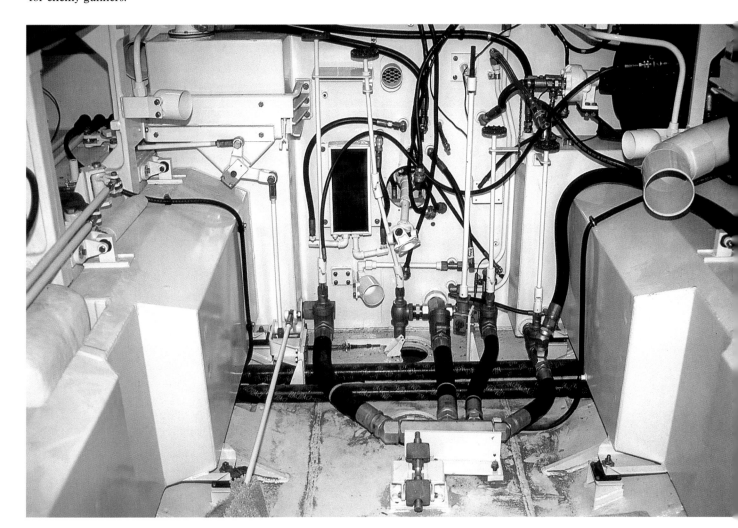

Power Pack

Tanks are tremendously heavy vehicles, even in World War II often weighing more than 60,000 pounds (27,200kg - more than 26 tons), and often more than twice that today. Moving that mass across country demands really big engines and transmissions.

In the 1930s-40s unorthodox solutions were sometimes tried: early Shermans used an aircraft engine, the 400hp Wright/Continental R975 radial **(see photo)**. The later M4A4 Sherman had its hull lengthened to take a huge 445hp Chrysler Multibank made up of five car engines geared to a common drive. Modern tanks use massive 700hp or bigger power-plants, generally diesels; the 1,500hp gas turbine engine of the M1 Abrams remains unique. (**Opposite above & below:** modern US air-cooled tank diesels in the 1,000hp range.)

Historically, ease of access for mechanics got a low priority when fitting available engines into tank hulls; and even today you generally can't see much of the engine when it is installed, even with the access panels open (see Soviet PT-76, **photo left**). Modern tank engines are therefore designed for relatively quick and simple removal. Some slide out on rails, although most have to be lifted out with a jib-arm on a wrecker or recovery vehicle in the field, or a hoist back in the motor pool. Electrical, fuel, air, control linkage and hydraulic lines are all fitted with quick-disconnects to simplify the job of extracting an engine in one piece; and although never less than a major job, it is now possible (under good conditions) to make a complete engine change in only an hour or two.

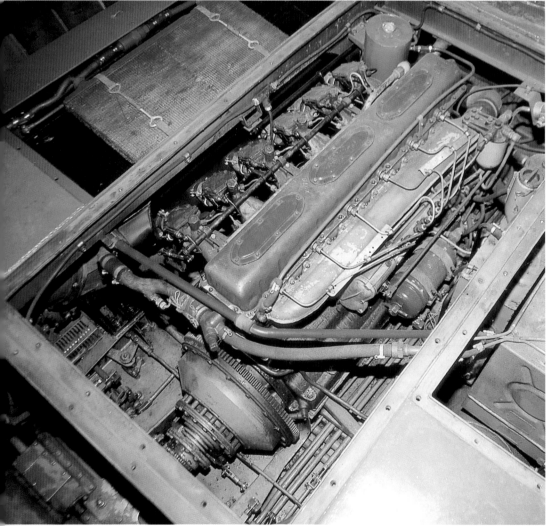

Suspension

The only way a vehicle weighing 30 to 60 tons can move across country without sinking to its belly is by distributing the weight over a fairly large surface - the tracks. The "footprint" of a motor car - the surface where the weight of the vehicle is in direct contact with the road - might be less than one square foot; the footprint of an M60 tank is about 67 square feet. A tank's ground pressure is often only ten or twelve pounds per square inch (psi).

The drive is transmitted to a toothed sprocket wheel, usually at the front, which moves ("lays") the track, fed forward over an "idler" wheel at the rear of the run and sometimes supported by "return rollers" along the top of the run. Road wheels, mounted either independently to torsion bar suspensions, or in pairs on bogies with spring or hydraulic shock absorbers, transmit the weight of the tank to the track.

(Opposite top) M5A1 Stuart: the nut on this rear idler arm adjusts track tension. Each track plate is attached to the next by hinge-type pins, and kept aligned with the wheels by tooth-like extensions. The 11.5in wide tracks give the 15-ton M5A1 a ground pressure of 12.5psi.

(Opposite bottom) M4A1 Sherman: these 16.5in wide tracks, with 12.25ft of ground contact, gave the 28-ton Sherman a high ground pressure of about 14psi - inferior to many German types, and a problem in "soft going".

(Above) From late 1944 Shermans were built with a new 23in wide track and this "horizontal volute spring suspension", reducing ground pressure to 11psi.

(Left) M60A1 Patton suspension: the pairs of rubber-tyred roadwheels are supported on individual torsion bars passing right across inside the belly.

(Right & below) Russian T-34: note rear-mounted drive sprocket, and Christie-type independent suspension with full-height double road wheels. The T-34 had excellent floatation in mud and snow; 19in-wide "waffle iron" track plates gave early models a ground pressure of only 9psi despite a weight and "footprint" length almost identical to the Sherman.

Track and suspension components are quite massive and durable, and can be difficult to work on when they do need fixing. "Breaking" a track in the field, to replace a damaged track plate while perhaps mired in mud or sand, is not an enjoyable job. Replacing a whole thrown track, by means of crowbars, cable and winch, is a long, back-breaking, finger- and toe-crushing ordeal for the whole crew.

(Left) The tracks of the British World War II Churchill had a very high top run - reminiscent of the original World War I tanks - to give good trench and obstacle crossing capability. The road wheels were mounted in 22 small, independently sprung bogies.

(Below) The German Hetzer was built on the basic chassis of the "Panzer 38t" - an excellent Czechoslovakian tank taken over by the occupying German forces. The tall steel road wheels provide a measure of extra side protection; and the Germans made great use of additional "skirt" plates hung along the sides of their AFVs.

Chapter 2
World War II: Matilda

Hard as it may be to believe today, in the first two years of World War II the little 26-ton Matilda II, armed with a 2-pounder (40mm) gun and with an effective cross-country speed of less than 10mph, was considered a heavy tank - and a seriously dangerous opponent for the best tanks then fielded by other armies.

Under the stimulus of war, developments in tank design advanced at frantic speed during 1941-45; and by the end of the war tanks like the German King Tiger, US Pershing and Soviet Josef Stalin were unrecognizably superior to the best equipment of 1939-40. But during the 20-year peace following World War I designers and tacticians had only been able to base their work on guesses about the shape of future wars; and the relative success of tanks like the Matilda in 1939-40 showed that they got at least some things right.

The theory in the 1930s - based on World War I experience - was that Britain needed three types of tank: "Light", for reconnaissance; fast, medium-weight "Cruisers" for exploiting break-throughs by the armored divisions; and slow, heavily armored "Infantry" tanks to support infantry assaults on fortified defenses. The result was over-complex production: too many different types were built, in too small numbers, and in the fast-moving campaigns of early World War II there were never enough tanks of the right type at the place and time they were needed. The Cruiser tanks proved, in any case, too weakly armored to take on the Panzers.

However, during the British Expeditionary Force's generally disastrous retreat to Dunkirk in May-June 1940, the first few Matilda IIs available to 7th Royal Tank Regiment gave the Germans - in the shape of the infantry, artillery and armor of Gen.Erwin Rommel's 7th Panzer Division, and the SS-Totenkopf Division - a severe fright. At Arras on 21 May, 7th RTR launched a counterattack across Rommel's fast-moving, strung-out columns; of 58 British tanks just sixteen were the new Matilda IIs, with the same 2-pdr. gun as the British Cruisers - but with armor protection up to a maximum of 78mm (3ins). So badly did they maul the Wehrmacht that 7th Panzer sent in a panicky report about attacks by "hundreds of

tanks"; in all they lost 30 to 40 AFVs and some 600 men. Under the general conditions of the Allied retreat this local victory could not be exploited; but examination of abandoned Matildas after Dunkirk gave the Wehrmacht plenty to think about.

The Matilda next went into battle in the North African desert in winter 1940/41, where a British Commonwealth army of just 36,000 faced about 250,000 Italian troops. A single regiment with a starting strength of less than 50 Matildas (rapidly "written down" by disabling minor damage as the battle progressed) spearheaded Operation Compass, Gen.0'Connor's offensive against several Italian divisions dispersed in fortified camps around Sidi Barrani and Bardia. In continuous close-quarter fighting the Matildas stormed through the Italian defenses, smashing the enemy's artillery and tanks and clearing a path for the following infantry. So complete was 0'Connor's victory - against huge odds - that at one point a British officer, asked to estimate the number of prisoners taken so far, radioed the reply that there were roughly "20 acres of officers and 100 acres of men". Not one Matilda was destroyed by enemy gunfire; their armor was proof against the worst the Italians could throw at them.

The appearance of the deadly German 88mm anti-tank gun in the desert during spring 1941 began the decline of the "Queen of the Battlefield"; it could punch through even the Matilda's carapace (though a hit did not always mean a kill: in June 1941 one Matilda of 4th RTR drove out of battle under its own power, with crew unwounded, after taking three 88mm hits). Although it was to be the end of that year before up-gunned and up-armored Panzer III Js could face the Matilda with any confidence, Rommel's Afrika Korps was tactically superior, and often made lethal use of screens of anti-tank guns to decimate British armor before tank-vs.-tank battles could develop.

Thereafter the gun/armor competition between German and Allied tank designers quickly took the state of the art a whole generation beyond the limits envisaged in the 1930s; and the survivors of the 3,000-odd Matildas built were used as the basis for various engineer vehicles.

Twin AEC diesel engines (174hp combined), radiators, gearboxes and fuel tanks are housed in the rear hull. Drive is to rear sprockets; ten small road wheels each side are mounted in sprung bogies. The suspension is protected by distinctive 25mm armor skirts with chutes to prevent mud clogging inside, and access doors for working on the bogies. The external drum on the rear hull is a 36-gal. auxiliary fuel tank. Official road speed was governed down to 15mph, but experienced comanders saved wear and tear by keeping below even that when they could; off-road radius of operation was about 80 miles.

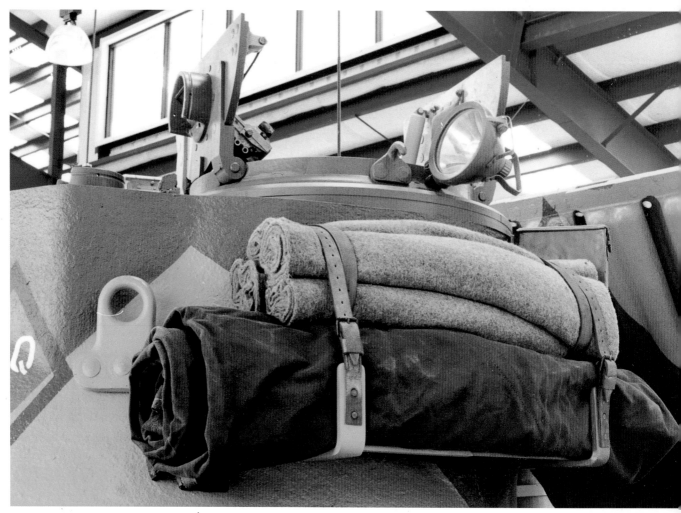

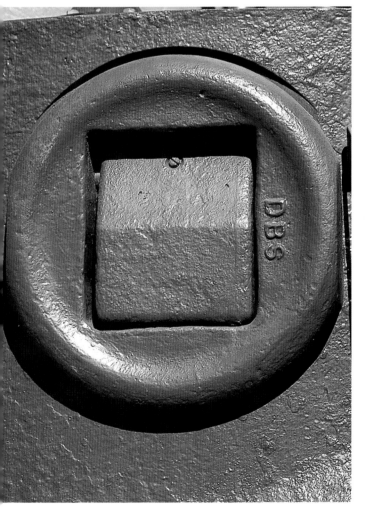

(Opposite top) The 2-pdr. gun, standard armament for British tanks in 1939-41, mounted in the cast steel turret (75mm armor). At the time its armor-piercing round could penetrate the 30mm armor of the Panzer III at 500-800 yards' range, while the Matilda was proof against the Germans' short 50mm gun. The main weakness of the 2-pdr. was that it only fired solid AP shot. Lack of a high explosive round made it ineffective against concealed gunpits, and against infantry - though the latter were often engaged at short range with the co-axial 7.92mm Besa machine gun, missing here, whose muzzle was normally seen in the rectangular port left of the main gun.

Left) "Pistol port" in left rear of turret, actually used for dumping empty shell cases.

(Opposite bottom) Stowage on the left turret brackets was supposed to include tarpaulin covers and camouflage netting, a bivouac tent, and the crew's bedrolls. Note also the commander's cupola, with two-part hatch open and periscope set in forward half; and open engine cover leaning against turret.

(Above) Right side of turret. Note smoke generators; behind them, magazine box for the Bren LMG sometimes carried for anti-aircraft defense; above, opened loader's hatch. British squadron markings were a triangle (A Sqn.), square (B Sqn.), circle (C Sqn.), or this diamond for Regimental HQ.

((**Above**) 78mm cast steel hull front - it's an easy tank to climb up. Note driver's position, with periscope and direct vision block, and mirror mounted on a rod. Two external lockers flank the driver's station - note latches, just above headlights. That on the left (as viewed) held cleaning kit, tools, spare track pins, etc.; that on the right, the crew's coats, packs, rations, cooking gear, and air recognition panels. Individual tank names beginning with D - here, Dunkerque, painted across the nose - identified 4th RTR.

(**Left**) Each regiment in a British formation had a code number, painted in contrasting colours on the nose. The traditional white/red/white British national recognition flash (first used in World War I) was also ordered painted on for Operation Crusader in November 1941; the crews hated it - it made too good an aiming mark for enemy gunners.

(Left) Spare track plates are clamped to the forward track covers. The driver's station has a curved, padded overhead plate which is rotated forward and back by internal levers. During the June 1941 fighting one 4th RTR driver's hatch was jammed open by repeated hits. Several more AP shot hit the mantlet above him during the day's fighting, and each time he got a shower of white-hot "spall" on his head and shoulders.

In the weird light conditions of the featureless desert the British tried several camouflage schemes, often based on naval-style "dazzle" with hard diagonal edges; colours seen striped over the pale sand base included this "silver-grey" and green, but also black-grey, tan, rust and purple-brown.

(Below) The black-on-white jerboa sign of 4th Armoured Brigade (comprising 4th and 7th RTR) within 7th Armoured Division.

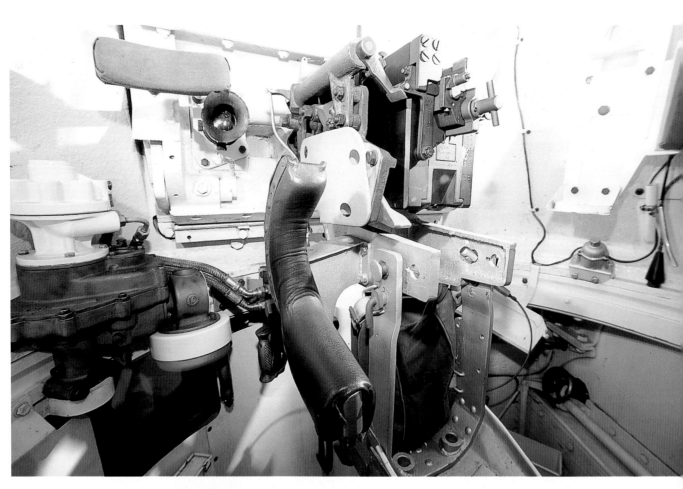

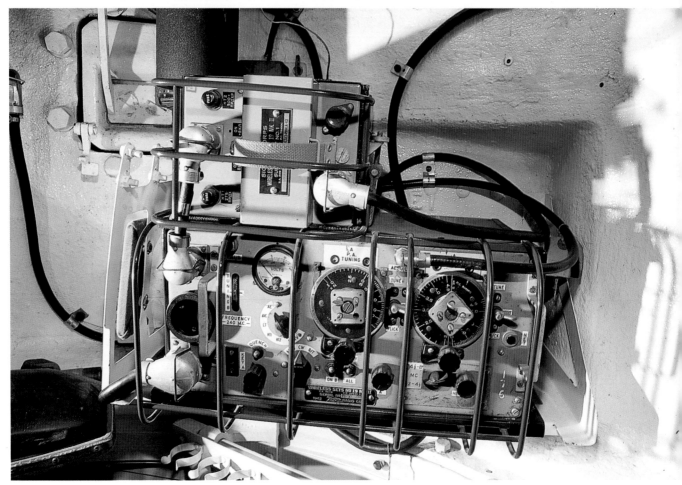

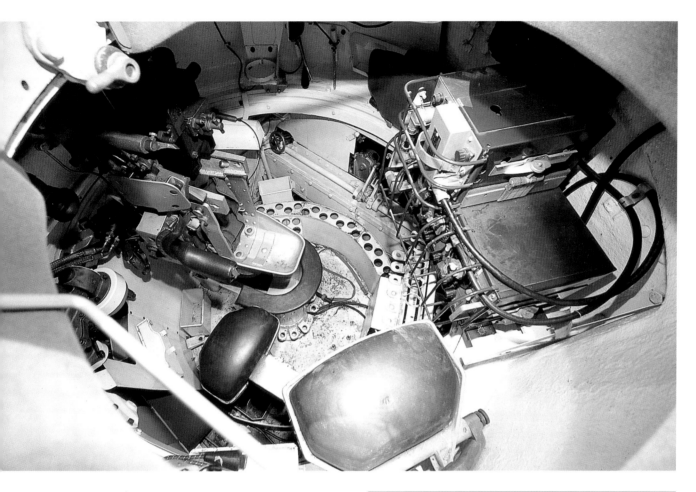

(Opposite top) Gunner's position on left of 2-pounder. Note telescope sight, centre; traverse control, left; and shoulder brace - the gunner leant into this to adjust elevation against friction dampers. Although the 2-pdr. was noted for its accuracy, this arrangement meant that it had to be layed anew after each shot.

(Left) The radio, mounted in an assymetrical space in the turret rear and protected by a cage. Early Matildas carried the No.11 set, later examples this No.19 set. It comprised an A-set for normal use, a B-set for close range comms, and an intercom C-set. Remembering which switch to use in an emergency was not always easy, and many veterans recall giving careful tactical reports to their driver while screaming at their squadron commander to go left....The No.19 set was also very noisy, and hours of listening to voice and Morse transmissions, static and mush could give you a severe headache.

(Above) Looking down through the commander's hatch into the three-man turret. With shells, MG ammo boxes, and many other normally stowed items absent here, it looks a lot more spacious than it was. Note the ejected case shield behind the gun breech, unfastened here to hang down - in action it would be rotated up 90 degrees, cutting the space in half. The gunner's and commander's seats are left and right foreground, the loader/operator's folded up just left of the radio. In all 93 racked rounds of main gun ammo could be carried.

"The Queen of the Battlefield": 7th RTR in the Western Desert

The Matildas of 7th Royal Tank Regiment spearheaded Gen.O'Connor's Operation Compass in December 1940/February 1941, against vastly larger Italian forces in a complex of positions around Sidi Barrani, Bardia and Tobruk on the Egyptian/Libyan border. After careful training and rehearsal, Lt.Col."Smoky Stover" Jerram's tanks, working with single brigades of Indian and Australian infantry, stormed a series of Italian positions with divisional-sized garrisons defended by plentiful artillery and armor.

Within four days O'Connor's 30,000-strong corps had taken or destroyed 237 guns and 73 tanks and captured 38,000 prisoners. The capture of Bardia on 5 January brought another 38,000 prisoners; that of Tobruk on the 22nd, 25,000, 208 guns and 87 tanks; and of Beda Fomm on 7 February, 20,000 men, 200 guns and 120 tanks (to no more than 3,000 Commonwealth troops engaged). The Matildas of 7th RTR were the key to many of these victories, and the tank was christened "Queen of the Battlefield". Although many were temporarily disabled by mine or gunfire damage to tracks and suspension, or shell splinters jamming the turret ring, there were no penetrations of the turret or hull (one Matilda crew counted no less than 38 shell scars on their armor), and personnel casualties were minimal.

Spring 1941 brought the German Afrika Korps to the desert; and although the Matilda was superior to the Panzer II and a match for the early Panzer III and IV, the long 50mm gun of later variants and, particularly, the 88mm anti-tank gun would end its dominance - gradually. Just nine 4th RTR Matildas handled 160 of Rommel's tanks so roughly at Halfaya Pass in June 1941 that three German senior officers were dismissed their commands. The Matildas of 4th, 42nd and 44th RTR still fought in the successful relief of Tobruk the following winter.

American-built scout cars and halftracks served and fought alongside tanks in many World War II campaigns, in the US and several Allied armies. They equipped the armored division's vital reconnaissance elements; they served as battlefield command, communications, and ambulance vehicles; they carried the armored infantry, and towed or mounted the support weapons, without which advancing tanks are fatally vulnerable to ambush. Indeed, the US M2/M3 halftrack series proved so versatile that it became more or less an all-purpose AFV, modified to fulfill dozens of roles; it was one of the most successful of all World War II armored vehicles, with more than 40,000 built between 1941 and 1945. They survived in many armies all over the world for decades, and a few were still in front line service in Israel and Vietnam at the end of the 1960s.

The White Scout Car - final designation, M3A1 - was developed by the Ordnance Department during the 1930s as an armored reconnaissance car for the US Cavalry. It served, basically as a rugged road vehicle, throughout World War II with US and Allied armies; but its four-ton weight, high ground pressure, relatively under-powered 110hp Hercules engine and two-wheel drive gave it an unimpressive cross-country performance, and its protection was inadequate for a true "battle taxi". From the late 1930s the US Army studied possible halftracked developments; the halftrack's great virtue was that it could accompany the tanks (almost) wherever their mission took them, so the complementary strengths of infantry and tanks need not be separated.

Various experimental models during the 1930s culminated in late 1940 in contracts for parallel production of two very similar but not identical halftracks: the "Car, Halftrack, M2", and the "Carrier, Personnel, Halftrack, M3". The most obvious differences were the M2's slightly shorter body, with a machine gun rail running round its rim as on the scout car, and no rear door; and the M3's longer body (and thus greater

Scout Cars & Halftracks

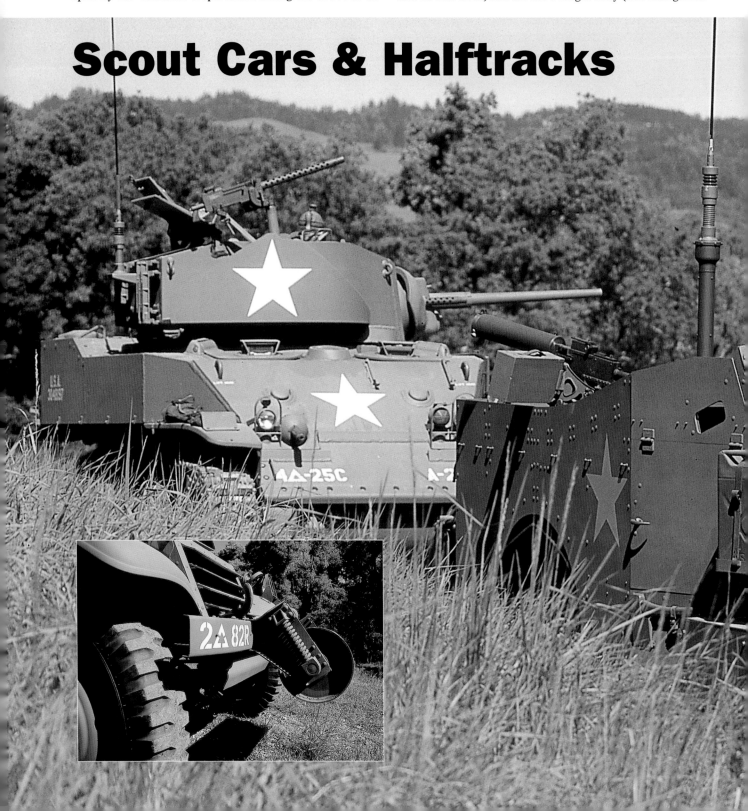

crew capacity), with a central rear door, and a "pulpit" machine gun position above the cab. Both lines would be produced by a number of companies, in models with slightly differing details and designations; retrospective modifications would further complicate the picture - in all more than 70 distinct models were built.

By 1943 the M3 and its derivatives were favored over the M2 series, and were the types mostly issued to the armored infantry. They could carry 13 men (i.e. a 12-man rifle squad and a driver), so five could lift a complete platoon of an MG squad, a mortar squad, and three rifle squads.

Nearly all the armor on the scout car and halftrack was only a quarter-inch thick, giving protection against rifle and light automatic fire and shell splinters; but the first GIs to take them into battle in Tunisia had over-optimistic ideas about them, which were quickly shaken by experience. The open hulls naturally gave no protection against artillery airbursts or any kind of plunging fire, and the side armor could be pene-

trated by anything heavier than infantry weapons. The mechanized infantry in armored divisions would suffer very heavy casualties; but this was later proved to be due to their heavy "workload" - being mobile, they were simply committed to combat more often than foot-slogging infantry.

White M3A1 scout car, typically teamed up with a Stuart light tank in the recon role. The national star was displayed by the Armored Force in yellow during 1942, and blue drab serial numbers from 1941. Used as a command car, this M3A1 has two radios installed.
(Inset) The sprung roller fitted to many scout cars and halftracks was to help prevent them "rooting in" when they went nose-down in ditches or against steep banks.

Even when the hull was not full of radios and other gear the scout car was cramped; it was officially supposed to seat six men in the rear, but this was always optimistic. Maximum road speed was 55mph. This M3A1's bumper markings identify 2nd Armored Division, 82nd Reconnaissance Battalion, Company A, car 1.

The only armor thicker than a quarter-inch (6.35mm) on all these vehicles was the half-inch (12.7mm) steel used for the sliding plates inside the door shields, and the armored windshield which could be lowered over the glass, or propped up as here. The movable armored slats over the radiator were not a successful solution to the conflicting needs for cooling and protection, and vehicles were often disabled when their radiators were pierced by gunfire or shell splinters.

Interior details of the M3A1 cab, with its simple instruments and uncomfortable seats. Note **(above)** how the skid rail for the machine guns curves up inside the cab area, with a padded canvas cushion strapped on above the door to prevent the driver braining himself.

Despite its drawbacks, nearly 21,000 M3A1s were built in 1939-44, and it was used by the British, Canadian and Russian armies as well as the US. In the counter-insurgency role it soldiered on in French Algeria into the early 1960s.

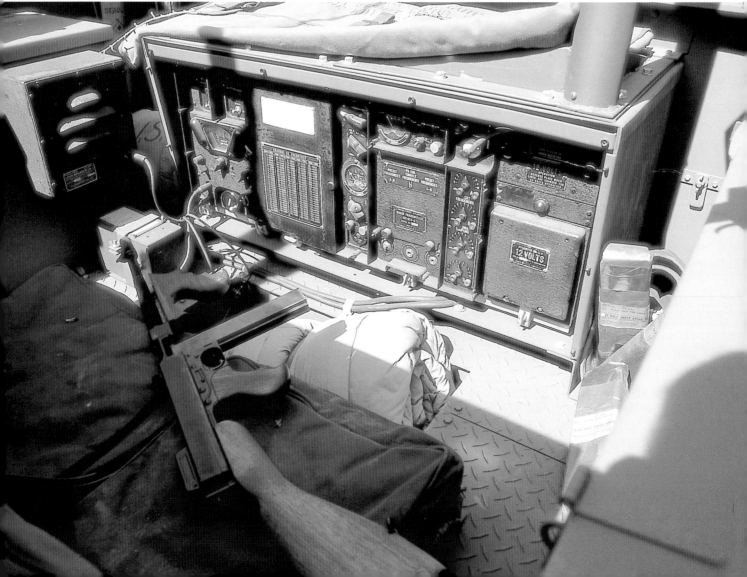

(Opposite top) The Browning M2HB .50cal air-cooled heavy machine gun could take on anything except tank armor; this sliding "skate" mount ran around the rail welded inside the scout car (and M2 halftrack) hull. Temporarily clamped above the cab, it has a canvas bag to catch the empty cases. (Above) Early in the war the water-cooled Browning M1917A1 .30cal was also seen on such vehicles. Note details of the skate mount; hauling a gun round the rail on this made rapid tracking or changing targets difficult.

(Left & right) This scout car has command radios fitted in the front and rear of the hull, with two back-facing seats. Many different combinations were used, including the SCR499 & SCR542. Note spare batteries, .45cal Thompson SMG, sleeping bag in the foot well, etc.; in the field even more clutter than this would be typical.

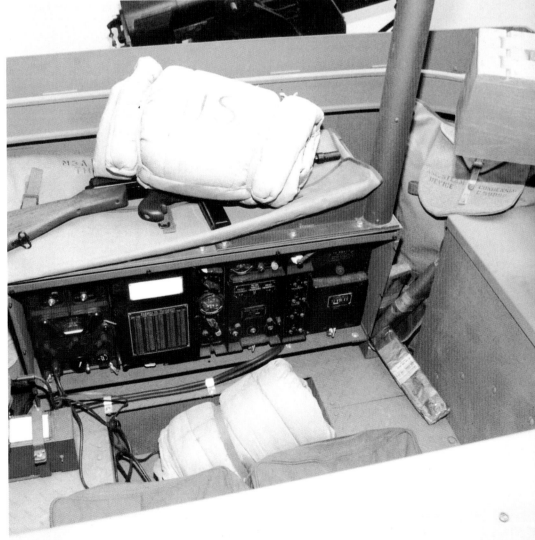

(Above & left) The rear hull of the M3A1 shows the construction: face-hardened armor plate bolted to the body frame. This beautifully stowed example is complete with the supports for the canvas tilt sometimes fitted over the body; and tripod mounts, allowing the .50cal and two .30cal guns to be dismounted for ground firing.

(Above right) This halftrack towing a 75mm gun is marked as belonging to the 4th Armored Division's 22nd Field Artillery. Confusingly, it is an M2A1 version - an M2 later partly modified to M3 standard, with the hull gun rail replaced by a "pulpit" over the cab. The ringed white star on the upper surface was adopted in 1943 as the standard Allied air recognition symbol.

(Right) The 12.75in-wide tracks are a single moulding of tough rubber over steel reinforcing cables, each with a "footprint" just under 4ft long, giving ground pressure of 11.3psi - better than a mid-war Sherman tank, and giving good floatation on soft ground. Track drive is via the front sprocket; the tension can be altered by adjusting the rear idler wheel. Both the front wheels and the tracks are powered; on good surfaces the front drive is disengaged and the tracks alone are powered, but for "loose going" the front axle drive is also engaged. Tests against captured German SdKfz 251 halftracks showed that the US type had far better mobility and steering over rough terrain, giving a better and quieter ride.

Halftrack Road Report

With an empty weight of just under eight tons, the basic halftrack APCs have a top road speed of 45mph; fuel consumption is a little better than three miles to the gallon, and range between 180 and 215 miles. They drive very much like a modern four-wheel-drive off-road vehicle - on which the power steering has failed.... The controls for the driver are absolutely conventional, and almost anybody could drive one on the road with minimal training. Operation off-road is a bit more of a challenge, particularly in soft going. Incidentally, all these light armored vehicles vibrate like hell and are extremely noisy - loose bits of iron clank and rattle all over, even without a load of GIs and their kit and weapons, and would-be drivers are advised to carry plenty of aspirin. Veteran armor officer *Duane Klug* comments:

"The halftrack is a bear to steer at low speeds, although it's not bad once you get it moving. As long as the front wheels aren't engaged, it will move along pretty well and is pretty easy to control. But once you engage the front axle it becomes much less responsive. I had to learn to double-clutch it, but if everything is set up right it drives like a regular transmission. It has a surprisingly good turning radius [59ft]. Visibility is good, as long as the armor windshields are up and the side curtains are down. It shakes the heck out of you, though."

The data plate reads:

```
CAR, HALF TRACK M2A1
WAS CAR, HALF TRACK M2
ORDNANCE DEPT. U.S. ARMY
CONVERTED BY        THE ORDNANCE DEPT.
MFGRS. SERIAL NO.   M2      5947
ORD. SERIAL NO.     M2      5947
ALLOWABLE GROSS WEIGHT        19,600    LBS.
      MAX. PAYLOAD INCL. STOWAGE
W/ROLLER   5000       W/WINCH    4500
MAXIMUM TOWED LOAD    4500 LBS.
MAX. SPEED 40 M.P.H. OR 3000 ENGINE R.P.M.
      PRESCRIBED BY USING SERVICE
OCTANE RATING OF GASOLINE   80
S.A.E. GRADE OF OIL      BELOW 32° F    10
S.A.E. GRADE OF OIL      ABOVE 32° F    30
PUBLICATIONS — PARTS LIST   SNL—G   102
OPERATORS MANUAL TM9  710
MAINT. MANUAL TM9  1710.  1710 C.  1711
```

(Left) About 5,000 M2 half-tracks were rebuilt, from October 1943, as M2A1s with the new M49 gun pulpit; but from this angle the shorter hull remains noticeable. See also one of the two big interior stowage boxes just behind the cab, and the outside access door to the nearside box. It was these which reduced the space for men; officially the M2 could carry ten, but in fact its size (and lack of rear doors) limited its use to such roles as a command or recon vehicle, prime mover for artillery, or carrier for machine gun and mortar squads, which were smaller than rifle squads.

(Top) The data plate in the M2A1 cab.

(Opposite top) One of the unprimed anti-tank mines sometimes carried in the hull racks, for the crew to use when consolidating captured ground.

(Above & right) One half-track modification was the M16 Multiple Gun Motor Carriage, with a Maxson turret mounting quad .50cal Brownings. Some 3,500 were produced from May 1943 as mobile light anti-aircraft defense for armored units. The relative scarcity of enemy ground-attack aircraft from mid-1944 led to the M16 "Meat-chopper's" awesome firepower being applied in the ground support role. Note the cut and hinged-down upper hull plates, to give the guns more depression. The M16 served on for many years; this one bears the markings of the 2nd Infantry Division's 82nd Anti-Aircraft Auto Weapons Battalion during the Korean War, where the quad-50 tracks saw much ground fighting.

(Left) The upper armor flap on the cab doors of the scout cars and halftracks folds outwards when not "tactical", showing the sliding plate over the vision port.

(Above) Many late-production halftracks were fitted with a 10,000-pound-capacity winch in place of the sprung front roller - much more useful for keeping vehicles moving under the actual conditions of Europe in winter.

(Left) Inside the halftrack cab, left side - generally very similar to the scout car. The main gearbox has four forward and one reverse gears, and driving controls are conventional, but with extra shift levers for front wheel drive, transfer case high and low ratios, and - when the winch is fitted - power take-off.

(Opposite top) The halftracks are powered by a truck powerplant, the White 160AX six-cylinder L-head petrol engine rated at 147hp at 3,000rpm.

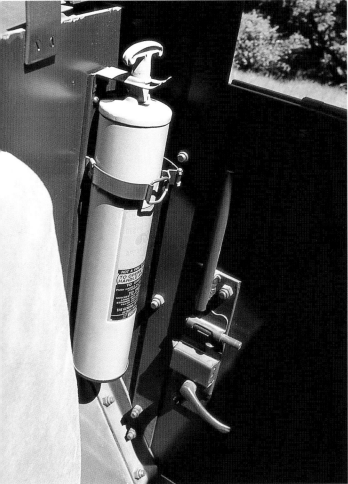

(Left & above) In theory, everything in a military vehicle has its proper place - from the fire extinguisher in the cab, to the bucket on the rear hull. In practice, of course, soldiers on campaign - enjoying the luxury of a halftrack rather than just a back-pack to stow their gear in - tended to acquire a huge variety of unofficial possessions.

World War II photos show a gypsy array of authorized and unauthorized weapons, munitions, bedrolls, stoves, pails, chairs, brooms, cartons, crates, sacks and bundles; some veterans even claim to have taken along hens for fresh eggs....

TO LOAD REEL

AMM. CHEST
CAL..50 M 2
200 ROUNDS

(Above left & above) The M45 Maxson turret fitted to the M16 (and similar M17) MGMC was electrically powered by a separate rear-fitted generator; the guns could traverse and elevate even when the halftrack's engine was switched off. The gunner wriggled into a seat between the two big circular trunnion plates.

(Far left) The sights were mounted on a bar above the central cut-out in the gunner's front armor plates.

(Left) The big 200-round ammo chests were wrestled into place by other crew members; the rounds alone weighed 50 pounds. Each gun had a rate of fire of between 450 and 575rpm, giving the M16 a firepower of around 2,000 rounds each minute - 500 pounds weight of metal.

US Armored Infantry Battalion, 1944

Headquarters Company
Bn.HQ (4 x jeeps, 2 x halftracks)
Co.HQ Platoon :
  HQ Section (1 ea. x jeep, halftrack)
  Maintenance Sect. (1 ea. x jeep, halftrack w.winch, 1-ton trailer)
  Admin., Mess & Supply Sect. (1 ea. x 2½-ton truck, trailer)
Recon Ptn. (5 x MG jeeps, 1 halftrack)
Mortar Ptn. (4 x halftracks, 3 x 81mm tubes)
Machine Gun Ptn. (3 x halftrack, 3 x .50cal MGs)
Assault Gun Ptn. (3 x M7 SP 105mm howitzers,
  2 x halftracks, 4 x ammunition trailers)

Service Company
(14 ea.x 2½-ton trucks, 1-ton trailers; 2 x ¾-ton trucks,
  3 x jeeps; 1 ea. x halftrack, 6-ton wrecker, M32 ARV)

Rifle Company (x 3)
Each 251 men, 20 halftracks:
HQ Ptn:
  HQ Sect. (1 ea. x jeep, halftrack)
  Maintenance Sect. (1 ea.x jeep, halftrack, 1-ton trailer)
  Admin., Mess & Supply Sect. (2 ea.x 2½-ton trucks, trailers)

Anti-tank Ptn. (1 x jeep, 3 ea.x halftracks, 57mm guns)

Rifle Ptns. (x 3), each:
  Ptn.HQ, & Rifle Squad as below (1 halftrack, . 50cal MG)
  Rifle Squads (x 2), each:
  1 halftrack, .30cal MG; 12 men; 1 ea.x .30 cal MG, bazooka)
  Mortar Squad (1 halftrack, 2 x 60mm tubes)
  Machine Gun Squad (1 halftrack, 1 x .50cal, 2 x .30cal MG)

M5A1 Stuart

The M3 Stuart light tank was rushed into production in 1941 as part of America's rearmament programme following the German triumph in France in 1940. It had a maximum armor thickness of 1.5ins (38mm), and an upright, boxy shape which at 8ft 3in high made a dangerously tall target. The two-man turret was cramped, with the commander having to double as gun loader and radio operator; at first it had only a hand-cranked traverse, and no turret floor, so the turret crew had to take care not to get their feet trapped as it turned. Its fuel consumption was high, limiting its radius of action to about 70 miles between refuelling stops.

Yet for all these apparent drawbacks, the hard-pressed British tankers who received it in the North African desert lovingly christened it the "Honey", and for several months used it - with more success than anyone had a right to expect - in the "Cruiser" role for tank-vs.-tank fighting. A tank's reputation among its crews depends not just on a cold comparison of technical specifications, but on what the crews have been accustomed to before, and what they face on the battlefield.

In early 1942 the Stuart's 37mm gun was good enough to knock out all Italian tanks; and most of the current German Panzers - if it could get to within 500 yards of them. Although the Stuart's flimsy armor put this well within the killing range of the German tank guns, its high speed and terrific manoeuvrability allowed battle-wise crews to get into

and out of action fast. A British Stuart commander who fought the Afrika Korps in November 1941 recalled:

"I worked out a system in my troop whereby, after the target had been indicated, a more or less automatic procedure followed....The object was to get close enough to the enemy tank to be able to destroy it. The first order, then, was 'Driver advance - flat out!' The gunner would do his best to keep his telescopic sight on the target all the time we were moving. The next order would be 'Driver - halt!' As soon as the tank stopped and he was on target the gunner would fire without further command from me. The sound of the shot was the signal for the driver to let in his clutch and be off again. From stop to start it took about four seconds."

British tanks had suffered a chronic rate of mechanical breakdowns in the desert, which often took many more tanks out of battle than enemy fire. The Stuart was not just a delight to drive; it was mechanically reliable, and easy to maintain and repair even in punishing desert conditions. Though it handled like a sports car, it never threw a track when racked around in a tight turn after biting off more than it could chew.

What's wrong with these pictures? Nothing - except that you would never see an armored fighting vehicle this clean and pretty out in the field. This particular M5A1 Stuart is a very special project, restored to virtually new condition both inside and out, and painted in the markings of the 25th Cavalry, a recon unit of the elite 4th Armored Division in 1944-45. The late turret has a distinctive armored shield around the external .30cal machine gun pintle on the right side.

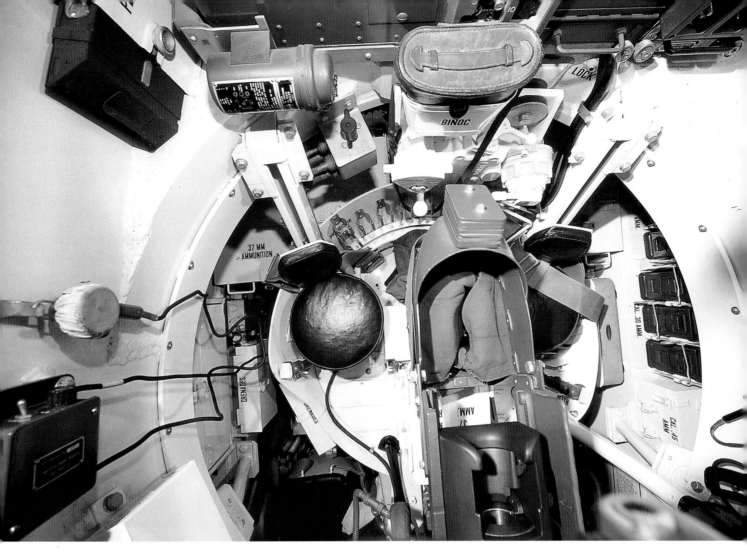

(Opposite top) M6 37mm gun mantlet, with co-axial .30cal MG. The 37mm armor-piercing round weighed 1.92 pounds; with a muzzle velocity of 2,900fps, it could penetrate 47mm of armor at 750 yards, 63mm at 100 yards. (We must perhaps view with scepticism the legend that a Stuart in a German forest in 1945 knocked out a Tiger by stalking it to point blank range from the rear and putting a round into the engine; the Tiger's rear hull plate was 80mm thick....) The gun fired AP, HE, smoke, and - unusually - a deadly anti-personnel canister round, which proved valuable to USMC tankers in the Pacific and British and Indian crews in Burma. Officially 147 rounds of 37mm could be stowed in racks and lockers, and 6,500 rounds of .30cal ammunition.

(Left) Unlike the co-ax gun, the .30cal Browning ball-mounted in the right side of the glacis and operated by the assistant driver could not be sighted - it was simply a "bullet hose", with some deterrent value to infantry at close range.

(Above) Looking down and back into the two-man turret of this beautifully restored M5A1; there is just room for the gunner (right as viewed) and commander (left). The latter also had to serve as the loader, and operated the radio (top,in the rear turret bustle); this was far too great a workload, distracting him from his command duties.

Marc Schring: "The crewmen in the turret are quite cramped, with small seats. Your knees are under the gun, up against the rounds in the ready rack. The hatches are poorly designed so it is tough to get in and out; buttoned up, you have no headroom at all. If you were in the turret you would get bruised constantly - lots of sharp corners and not much padding, with primitive ergonomics."

The Stuart was as popular in the Pacific theatre, where it was the only tank available to the US Army and Marines in their desperate early 1942 battles such as Luzon and Guadalcanal, and was still doing yeoman work on Eniwetok and the Admiralty Islands in early 1944. It was used to good effect by British and Indian crews fighting in Burma - as rearguards during the retreat of 1942, in the battles which smashed the Japanese advance around Imphal in early 1944, and in the triumphant offensive of spring 1945.

This later island and jungle fighting was usually carried out almost blind - often at less than 50 yards range, against concealed bunkers which sometimes mounted ordnance serious enough to take a heavy toll of the thinly armored Stuarts. But its gun was always a match for any Japanese tank encountered (these were few and far between, and usually very unskilfully handled). Its AP and HE rounds were used in deadly combination for "bunker-busting"; and its lethal canister "shotgun" rounds broke up many a banzai infantry charge, and swept treetops free of snipers.

From 1942 the M5 series offered many improvements, notably a better (though still cramped) power-operated turret, a better gun mount and optical equipment, and quiet, powerful Cadillac engines with automatic transmission. Outclassed in Africa and Europe by spring 1943, and thereafter replaced as a tank-fighter by the M4 Sherman, the Stuart still served on until the end of the war with the recon units of US and Allied divisions - where its agility and speed paid dividends - and in support of mechanized infantry. Nearly 20,000 Stuarts were built before production ceased in June 1944. Many hulls were also modified for various specialized tasks, mounting howitzers or flamethrowers.

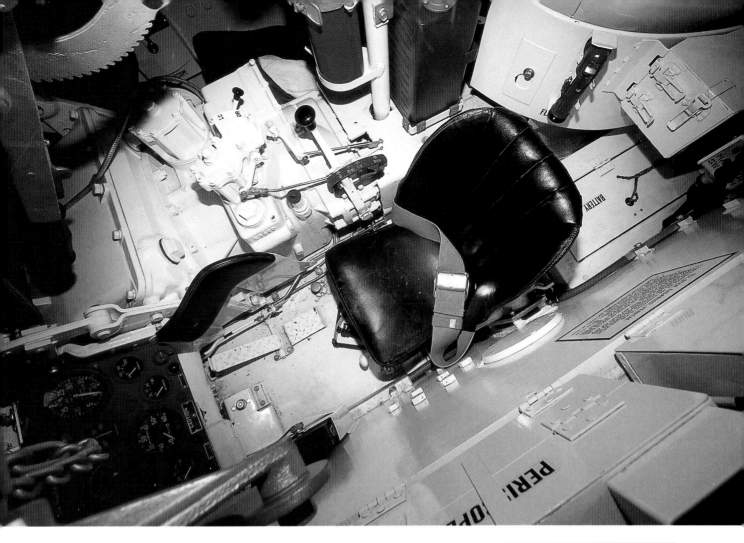

(Opposite top) Looking forward at the gunner's station. Extreme left, the traverse and firing control; the elevation wheel is visible on the left side of the gun mounting. The gunner has a periscope (top left, with white pad) for wide field vision and a telescope sight (center, grey pad, above co-ax MG ammo box) for aiming the gun, both linked to the tube. At top right note the commander's periscope.

(Far left) Gunner's control handle; the turret is traversed by rotating the black "spade" handle, and the co-ax .30cal and 37mm are fired by the two red buttons - the latter could also be fired by a foot pedal. A gyro-stabilizer was installed, holding the barrel elevation constant as the tank moved across rough terrain; but fire-on-the-move shooting was not really practical, and the compensating rise and fall of the gun breech in the cramped turret made life difficult for gunner and loader alike - the device was usually switched off.

(Left) Gunner's weapon control panel, on the left turret wall forward of the periscope.

(Above) The comparatively roomy driver's station at front left, seen through his hatch; the edge of the turret "basket" curves round behind his seat. (It was a design defect that the two front hull hatches had to be closed before the turret could traverse freely.) Steering was by selective braking of each track with two levers - invisible here, as in the M5 they were mounted to hang down from linkages across the roof rather than on the deck. The assistant driver/hull gunner had an unusual luxury, envied by the drivers of other tanks: a set of duplicate controls, so that he could take over from the driver on long road marches.

M5A1 Stuart Road Report

Marc Sehring: "The driving position in the Stuart is quite nice; the compartment is roomy, and the tank steers well. The automatic transmission makes it quite easy to drive, and the driver is the only really comfortable guy in the crew.... The Stuart is very fast, light, and quiet - other than the clunking of the tracks, you can have a hard time telling if the engine is running, even from inside! That makes it a great vehicle for scouting and reconnaissance - you could avoid or escape a dangerous situation even when you couldn't shoot your way out. If you step on the gas, it really picks up and goes." When the gas pedal is pushed down as far as it will go, it not only opens the throttle all the way; it also kicks the Hydramatic transmission into shifting down, giving excellent acceleration. Early M3 series Stuarts had Continental petrol or Guiberson diesel radial engines and synchromesh transmission; but the M5 series uses two Cadillac Series 42 V-8 car engines, each driving Hydramatic transmissions linked to the drive shaft, and developing 220hp at 4,000 revs. That's a lot of power for a 15-ton scooter - as long as the engines are properly synchronized. *Duane Klug*: "If the engines are not synchronized, you've got a problem; then you'll be grinding gears, and they'll overheat. But if they're set up right, it will run like a scalded ape!" Top speed is officially listed at 36mph.

M4A1 Sherman

The M4 Sherman was probably the most widely built and best-known tank of World War II. It was the standard battle tank of the US and the Western Allies from late 1942 onwards; some 55,000 were delivered to the US Army, and 26,000 served with Allied armies - 20,000 with the British, and even 5,400 with the Red Army. And - with apologies to any sentimental Sherman veterans - that may seem a little odd, since it wasn't outstanding in any department.

Although a definite improvement over earlier US and British types, and a good match for the German Panzer III and IV, the Sherman was inferior to the later Panzer V Panther and heavy Panzer VI Tiger in most respects - notably, in armor protection and gun penetrating power. Its narrow tracks gave poor floatation in soft going, and its tall silhouette made it stand out like a sore thumb. Thanks partly to the petrol engine, but mostly to the ease with which any penetration set off its racked shells, it had such a reputation for catching fire when hit that GIs called it the "Ronson" (guaranteed to light up at the first try...), and British tankers the "Tommy-Cooker", after their field stove.

But...it was simple, rugged, and mechanically reliable, and that's important on the battlefield. It had a good, fast traverse that could often give it the first shot in an engagement. It gave the Allies all the advantages of standardizing on a single basic design; US industry could turn them out in huge numbers to replace battle losses, while Germany never had enough Panthers and Tigers to equip more than about a third of the units facing them.

The US Army made a conscious decision in 1943: to ignore calls for rapid development of the heavy, 90mm-gun T26 (Pershing) to take on the Panthers and Tigers, and instead to mass produce the M4 - a medium tank that would do the job well enough rather than brilliantly, and at a practical cost in time, talent, treasure, and shipping weight.

Its 75mm gun and 50mm (2in) frontal armor were not good enough to take on a late Panzer head-to-head; but Sherman crews used their numbers, speed and agility to swarm round the Panthers and Tigers. The Panzer might survive long enough to kill one, maybe even two M4s; but in the meantime the rest of the platoon, working round onto its flanks, would be putting rounds into its more vulnerable sides and engine compartment from close up.

The Sherman also lent itself to adaptation. The 75mm gun was a good all-purpose weapon with a very useful HE round; but when its shortcomings against the new Panzers became evident, the British customized a proportion of their Sherman fleet by shoe-horning into the turret their big 17-pounder anti-tank gun. Probably the best Allied anti-tank weapon of the war, this 76mm (3in) gun could pierce at least 130mm of armour sloped at 30 degrees at 1,000 yards range, compared to about 60mm for the 75mm gun (the frontal armor of Tigers and Panthers was around 80mm). Sadly, there were never enough of these 17-pdr.Sherman "Fireflies" to issue more than one tank per platoon. The US Army turned them down, but late US Shermans received a new turret for the long 76mm M1 series gun (which actually gave little better penetration than the 75mm).

One good point about the US Sherman's guns was that their trajectory allowed indirect fire - wartime photos show tanks lined up track to track on slopes with guns elevated, firing HE barrages over crests like howitzer batteries, a tactic impossible for most German tanks with their high velocity cannon.

Of the many versions of the M4 which were produced, varying in armor, turret, ammo stowage, weapon, engine and suspension, the best - by acclamation - was the M4A3E8 ("Easy 8") with a big liquid-cooled V8 engine, wider tracks, HVSS suspension, and enlarged turret with 76mm gun; these began to reach the troops soon after D-Day. They served on for some years, seeing combat in Korea; and they - and many earlier marks - would continue to serve in overseas armies for decades afterwards. A handful served in Israel's 1948 war of independence, and many in her 1956 and 1967 campaigns; Shermans fought in the Indo-Pakistan wars of 1965 and 1971; and in odd pockets of the Third World a few may have soldiered on even later.

(Previous pages & opposite top) Cast hull M4A1 Sherman, here a 1942-vintage Canadian-built "Grizzly" version, marked for the 37th Tank Bn., US 4th Armd.Div., NW Europe, 1944. The welded-on side plate gives necessary extra protection to ammo racks inside; sadly, the white star also makes a perfect aiming point.

(Above) The rough-cast, 3.5in thick mantlet of the 75mm gun; note sight aperture, and .30cal co-axial MG, at left and right as viewed. (Right) A horribly easy kill for a Panzer: the turret rear armor is 2ins thick, the engine access doors about half that. The M4A1's Continental R975 air-cooled radial engine is powerful and, when well cared-for, dependable, but not without problems. A cold engine has to be rotated with a crank handle before starting, to lube the cylinder walls and preclude hydrostatic lock; the engine also has to be pulled out to get at the spark plugs on the lower end.

(Left) This M4A1 is retrofitted with the all-round-vision cupola which was factory-fitted during production from mid-1943. Note the bearings round the inner edge of the hatch, allowing the commander to rotate his periscope.
(Below) The M34A1 mantlet, traversing and elevating with the M3 75mm gun to shield the gap where it emerges from the turret front.

(Right) The hatches for driver and co-driver are a tight and awkward fit, especially for crewmen bundled in winter coveralls and wearing shoulder holsters; getting out of a "brewing" tank was a perilous business. Note the fixed periscope in front of the driver's station, and the rotating one in his hatch.

Sherman Combat Report

John Whitehill joined Able Co., 37th Tank Bn. as a green second-lieutenant after the battalion had been in combat for some weeks. The battalion CO, the legendary Col.Creighton Abrams (for whom the M1 tank is named) looked over the replacements he'd been sent and snarled, "If I wanted second-lieutenants I would have made some myself!" But John and the other replacements proved themselves soon enough. John had four M4s shot out from under him; despite their reputation, not one caught fire. John was wounded four times, and was awarded the Distinguished Service Cross for action at Bigonville, Luxembourg. A full-strength company in 1944 had 17 tanks; A/37 lost 32 during the war - nearly 200 per cent attrition. The normal tank company included five officers; Whitehill was the fifteenth officer lost when he was wounded by a Panzerfaust; and in all Able Co. would loose 176 men against an authorized strength of 117. It was, in other words, a bloody business.

"My first tank was destroyed when a German infantryman fired a Panzerfaust at us. It hit the turret broadside, and didn't penetrate the armor, but it sure shook us up; the noise was tremendous, sparks and smoke flew everywhere, and there was a smell that reminded me of brimstone. I backed the tank up about 200 yards into a woodline, but as I was backing a German tank hit me with armor-piercing rounds; one hit the left front of the tank, breaking the track and destroying a bogie wheel. We were able to back up the length of the remaining track, but that's all - we abandoned the tank.

"I lost my second in November 1944 while leaving a village. I was in the lead, and about 200 yards down the road I got hit by a German HE round on the left side of the tank. When I recovered, I looked to the left and saw three German tanks; but before I could do anything they fired again. I couldn't figure out what they were shooting at until I saw something fall into the field to my right - it was my gun tube! Well, we couldn't fire back, and we couldn't get off the road, so we abandoned that tank right there. My crew and I were sheltering in the gutter when the German tanks opened up from our front. One of the rounds struck my driver just as he was crossing the road, and he was killed instantly. The remaining four of us crawled back to the shelter of the village, and I took over another tank.

"I lost my third tank when I ran over a mine during the Battle of the Bulge. I thought I'd been hit by a tank round, and was searching frantically for the enemy when the sergeant behind me called on the radio telling me that it was a mine. It took out about four feet of track and the front bogie wheel, and caved in the bottom of the tank at the driver's position, injuring him. I was company commander by this time, the previous commanders having been killed or injured. I commandeered my sergeant's tank and told him to take care of my crew.

"Twenty minutes later I lost that tank, too, when I went over the brow of a hill: with just the turret exposed, I took three AP hits on the left-front corner of the turret. Again, there was a hell of a jolt, smoke, sparks, and the smell of brimstone. The impact knocked loose all the equipment bolted to the left interior wall of the turret, injuring the loader. More material from the turret ring race struck the driver, cutting him. The tank was idling when we got hit, but it was in gear; after we got hit the whole crew except me bailed out and started running to the rear. I realized the thing would still run, so I climbed down into the driver's compartment, turned it around, and caught up with the crew and asked them if they wanted a ride. The tank wasn't battle-worthy, so I fought the company on foot the rest of the day, using hand and arm signals to issue commands.

"On another occasion the loader and I were standing up in the hatch, scanning for targets, when a German round came between us, ricocheted off the turret, and decapitated the loader. He fell back into the turret, and the rest of the crew abandoned the tank - leaving me with an operable tank, no crew, and a dead man on the turret floor. The medics came up and we put a web belt around him under the armpits, and they pulled while I pushed from inside, and we got him out that way. I turned that tank over to my supply sergeant; he and his crew took GI soap and water and tried to clean it up as best they could, but he has never forgiven me...."

(Above) Driver's simple instrument panel on left of seat: big speedo and tacho dials, smaller gauges for ammeter, oil temperature and pressure, and fuel, triple switch (top center) for cranking engine and magnetos, and various circuit breaker reset buttons.

(Opposite top) Driver's position: black-gripped steering brake control levers ("laterals") between clutch and gas pedals; below and right of periscope, black knob of primer pump; below this on right of box, white-painted hand throttle; adjustable seat; right of this, knobbed gearshift lever and plain parking brake.

(Right) The large transmission housing between the driver's and bow gunner's stations (the latter's seat is removed here). Stowed above the transmission is a large collapsible canvas hood, complete with glass window and wiper; for use by the driver when driving "head out", this was generally too confining and cumbersome for use in the front lines.

(Opposite bottom) Bow gunner's station. The M1919A4 .30cal was - as in the Stuart - an unaimable "bullet hose", whose fire could in theory be corrected by orders from the commander observing bullet strike. Some main gun and MG ammo was stowed in the hull sponsons beside the two front crew stations. The floor escape hatch was fitted behind the co-driver's seat.

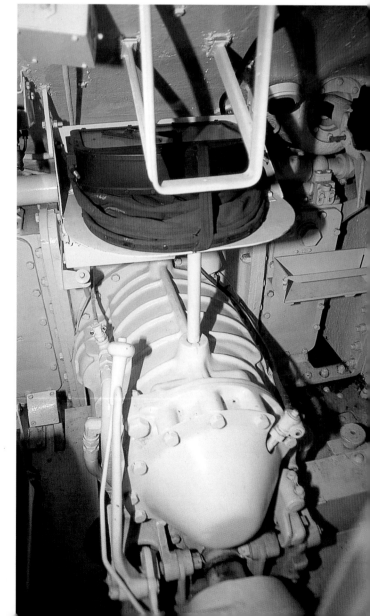

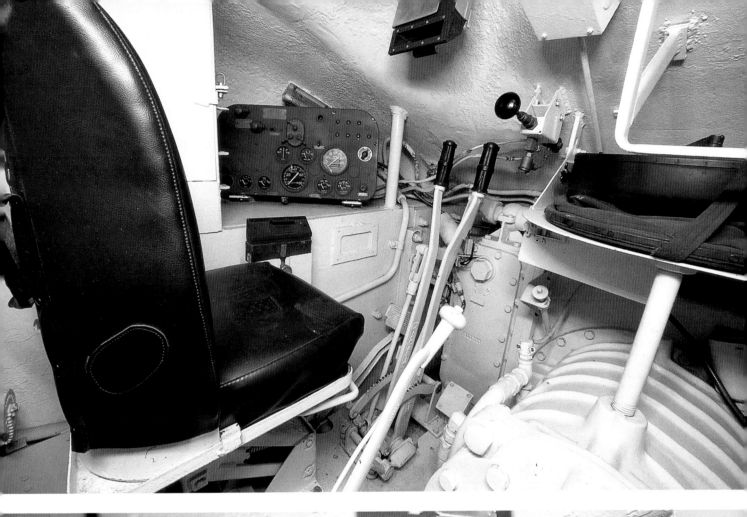
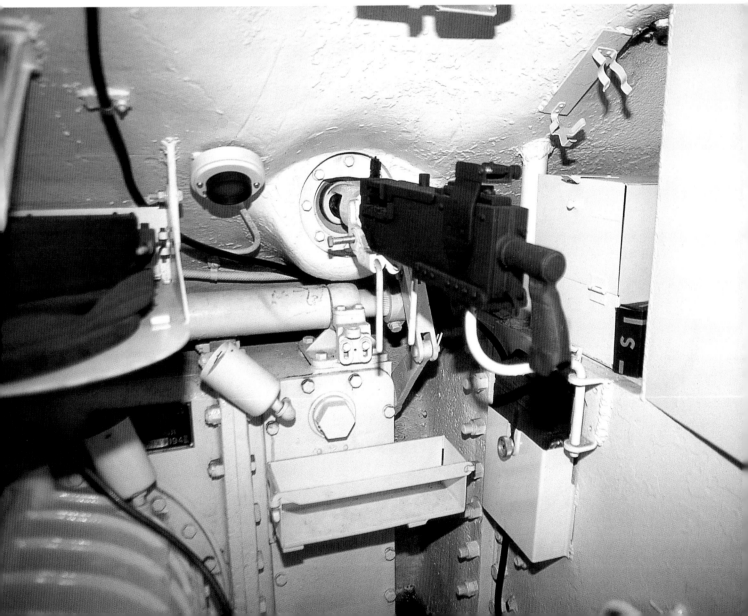

(Left) General arrangement view from rear of a "cutaway" Sherman demonstration turret, the cutaway edges painted red: loader's station left of gun breech, gunner's right, and TC's above and behind gunner.

(Below left) Loader's station, looking forwards: roof periscope, breech of 2in smoke mortar firing through roof, co-axial .30cal with ammo box in cradle.

(Below) Looking from left to right across the 75mm gun breech, from loader's to gunner's station. The co-axial .30cal is mounted left of the main gun and fired by this solenoid, actuated by the gunner on the far side of the breech.

Sherman Road Report

Marc Sehring: "The M4 Sherman is a weird design: that high silhouette seems like such a waste of space. It is pretty uncomfortable inside. The turret is a bit cramped, particularly for the commander and gunner but not too bad for the loader. The early Sherman were a noisy tank, rough-riding and not particularly manoeuverable. I have driven a lot of them, and some are easy to steer while others are very difficult. Visibility is poor, buttoned up.

"The radial engine isn't bad, as long as you keep it maintained - plenty of horsepower. It's pretty easy to maintain, close to the T-34 in simplicity. It uses some oil, but then they all did. It's a hell of a fire hazard, though, and you've got to have somebody standing there with a fire extinguisher whenever you start up. The little auxiliary engine is a nice touch, allowing you to run the radios without draining the batteries."

Dean Klefman: "I've crewed two versions of the Sherman, the M4A3E8 'Easy 8' and the 'Grizzly'. The Easy 8 is the Cadillac of the Shermans, a really fine tank; but it has one bad feature, and that's a half-basket. The turret basket on this model is only under the TC and the gunner; the loader stands on the hull floor when he isn't sitting down. Other than that, it's a great tank. You've got plenty of room, good periscopes, and the loader has his own hatch - unlike the earlier models.

"Starting is extremely simple: hop in, turn on the master power switch, hit the magnetos, hit the starter switch, and BOOM, that big Ford V8 kicks in! Very reliable, and plenty of power. The nice thing about driving the Easy 8 is that you sit up high, and you're not cramped. I'm 6ft 2in tall, and still have plenty of room. Normally, you start out in second gear; it's got five forward gears, but we seldom get it out of second or third. And you can drive it standing up, tapping the laterals with your elbows as required. Once you get it going in a straight line, it will keep going straight unless you tap one of the laterals. Shifting up is easy, but downshifting requires double-clutching.

"In winter it can be awfully cold. When that steel gets cold, you just can't get the thing warmed up again. Even with blanket coveralls and tanker's jacket, you can really get chilled....You get bounced around quite a bit going across open terrain, and I traded in my tanker's helmet for a steel pot for protection in the turret."

(Above) The usual radio mounted in the rear turret bustle was the SCR508, 528 or 538. Note covered Thompson gun and its magazines, top, and K-ration packs, left. (Left) Looking forwards into bow gunner's station from bottom of turret: MG ammo stowed on turret basket floor ahead of 75mm ammo ready rack.

(Opposite top) Eight-round ready rack on turret basket floor, looking left to right - various HE and AP types are shown here. Other official stowage was 12 rounds upright round the basket rim, 15 and 17 in left and right hull sponsons forward, 15 in right sponson aft, and 30 under the basket floor. In practice, as many rounds as possible were piled around the floor; Col.William Marshall's crew found the ready rack just the right size for bottles of wine....(Right) Auxiliary generator in left rear corner of the hull; this provided independent power for the radio and charging the batteries, and even a little warmth in winter.

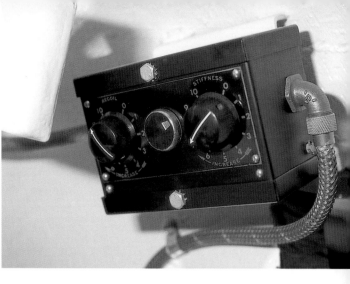

(Left) Looking down into gunner's station from commander's hatch: elevation and traverse controls ahead of flip-up seat, azimuth indicator (for use in indirect fire) to the right of it, periscope with white pad above controls - the telescope sight seems to be absent from this photo.

(Above) Gunner's recoil control box, mounted on turret wall right of periscope.

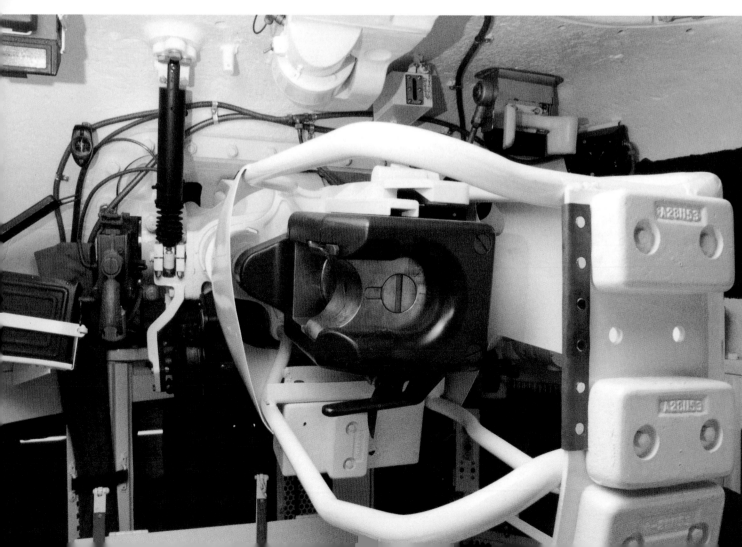

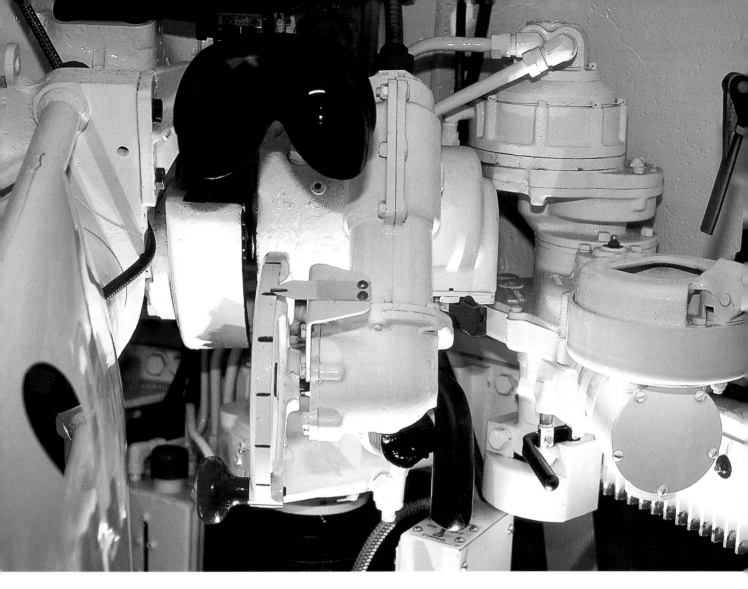

(Above) Looking forwards from gunner's seat: left, elevation control wheel, here with red-painted knob; above this, x3 M70 telescopic sight; center, black "spade" grip of power traverse, with reserve hand trigger - primary firing was by a foot pedal; right, lever of the manual traverse.

(Left) Looking forwards from left rear of turret at the M3 75mm gun in its M34A1 mount; note counterweights at the rear of the body shield which guarded the turret crew from the recoiling breech. Just visible beyond it on the right turret wall are lengths of brown padding, to cut down crew injuries; unfortunately, most were caused by heads and joints being thrown against protruding assemblies - which could not be padded, as they had to be accessible.

(Right) Cutaway turret, looking from right to left across the gunner's station: azimuth, traverse and elevation gear, telescopic sight, and periscope with slanting bar slaving it to the gun. At bottom left the open ammo ready rack can just be seen.

Access to the main ammo stowage under the turret basket floor was particularly awkward; some co-drivers reversed their seats to sit facing backwards, where they could more easily wrestle the 18- or 20-pound rounds out and pass them up through the gaps in the turret basket.

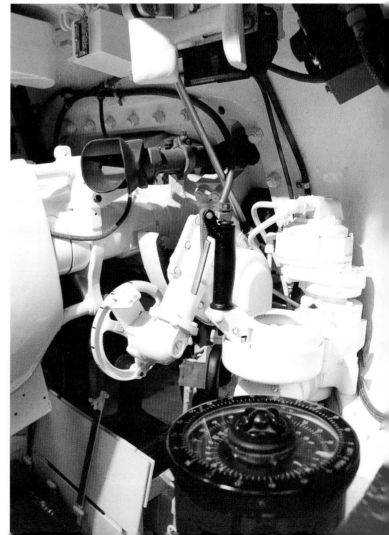

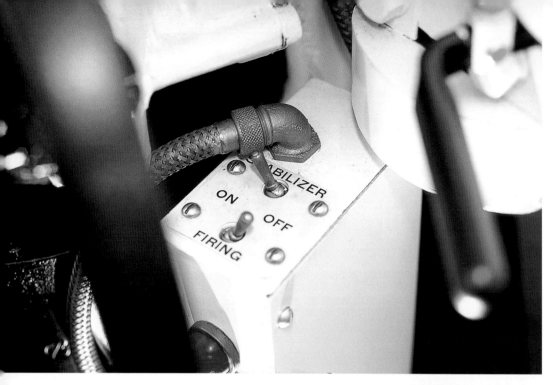

(Left) Controls of Oilgear gyro-stabilizer fitted to the Sherman's 75mm gun, beneath the power traverse handle. By stabilizing the angle of elevation of the gun on the move, this was supposed to allow firing without halting. Reports from crews varied: many disliked it and kept it switched off; some claimed it was useful if crews took the time and trouble to train thoroughly and maintain it carefully.

(Right) Looking from left to right underneath the gun breech at the gyro-stabilizer gear, in this case with a black-painted control box. Note also the gun trunnion, top center, and power traverse and elevation controls, right.

Jagdpanzer 38
Hetzer

As the war ground on, Germany - fighting on three fronts against huge odds - found it ever harder to keep up the supply of tanks to her front line divisions. One solution was greatly to increase the number of Jagdpanzer or Panzerjaeger - "tank-destroyers". These turretless AFVs, their guns mounted (with very limited traverse) in a fixed superstructure, were thought adequate for most defensive fighting - and in 1944 the Wehrmacht was fighting on the defensive almost everywhere. Without a complex traversing turret, the tank-destroyers were quicker and cheaper to build; their low profile made them easy to conceal in ambush; and the crews, drawn largely from the artillery, did not have to be so highly trained for battles of manoeuvre as the tank crews.

These tank destroyers appeared in many different models, using the basic chassis and running gear of existing German, French and Czech tanks; the 1944 Panzerjaeger 38 Hetzer (which loosely translates as "Troublemaker") was based on the excellent Czech Skoda 38, which Germany had appropriated in large numbers in 1939 after occupying Czechoslovakia. As a tank-destroyer it was given a low, boxy superstructure of sharply sloped armor, and mounted an excellent existing German gun, the 75mm L48 Pak 39.

Allied tank crews advancing into German-held territory became justifiably nervous of the Panzerjaegers, whose hidden presence was usually only betrayed when the first Sherman, Cromwell or T-34 in the column was suddenly struck, with a noise like a giant's hammer hitting an anvil, and burst into flames. But the tank-destroyers suffered from several major drawbacks, and once flushed from their hiding places they had no chance of surviving a moving fight with real tanks.

Their guns may have been powerful, but had such a limited range of motion in the slots at the front of their armored box bodies that initial aiming involved the whole vehicle - the commander had to direct the driver to align it with a road or valley down which the enemy were thought likely to appear,

and simply hope that they would arrive in front of him from the right direction. The gunner could make fine adjustments; but if the targets decided to move across the gun's front at a high angle it was almost impossible to track them and fire before having to move the whole vehicle. This compromised any camouflage and concealment - and also turned the thin side armor towards the enemy's counterfire. The Hetzer had the worst arc of traverse of any German SP gun: only five degrees left and 11 degrees right. Although the Hetzer's excellent chassis, engine and drive train earned it a reliable reputation, it suffered gravely from all these other drawbacks. These were summed up some years ago, in an article in *AFV News* by former Hetzer combat commander Armin Sohns. To summarise his comments:

The main problems stemmed from the off-center position of the gun, set in the right side of the body, which meant that three of the four-man crew had to be crowded into the left side - driver, gunner and loader in single file, from front to back. The commander was stuck at the right rear, behind the gun, in a small space carved out of the engine compartment. In this type of AFV, with its particular aiming problems, close co-operation between driver, gunner and commander is vital; separating the commander like this had a disastrous effect on efficient teamwork. Visibility was bad all round due to inadequate provision of periscopes; the commander, stuck so far back, had a huge blind area to his front unless he exposed himself dangerously, while the rest of the entombed crew were almost entirely dependent on his directions.

Using existing components to improvise a fighting vehicle may be cheaper, but it has many traps. All the breech controls of the existing Pak 39 gun were mounted on the right side, and the main ammo stowage also had to be on the right of the hull. The loader had to lean over the gunner and over the breech to reach them; and when the gunner traversed right, the breech moved left and pushed the loader even further away from them.

(Left) Slinking out of the treeline, the Hetzer shows a menacingly low profile - it is only seven feet high. Firing from ambush, it took a considerable toll of Allied AFVs in 1944-45; but it had serious built-in disadvantages.

(Right) Right front drive sprocket and apron armor. At only 16 tons, with broad tracks, the Hetzer had good floatation.

(Left) Rear hull. Note the hatch under the machine gun mounting - this is the only entrance and exit for the three crew members sitting on the left of the fighting compartment - and was only accessible when the MG was traversed sideways. The commander's hatch at the right rear corner is so small that it has to have two flaps, one in the roof and one in the sloping rear plate.

(Right) The rear hull plate. The muffler was originally set horizontally, but was modified when it proved a dangerous trap for anti-tank charges tossed onto the engine deck. The 6mm armor panel, at lower right of the top plate, is for access to the engine air filters.

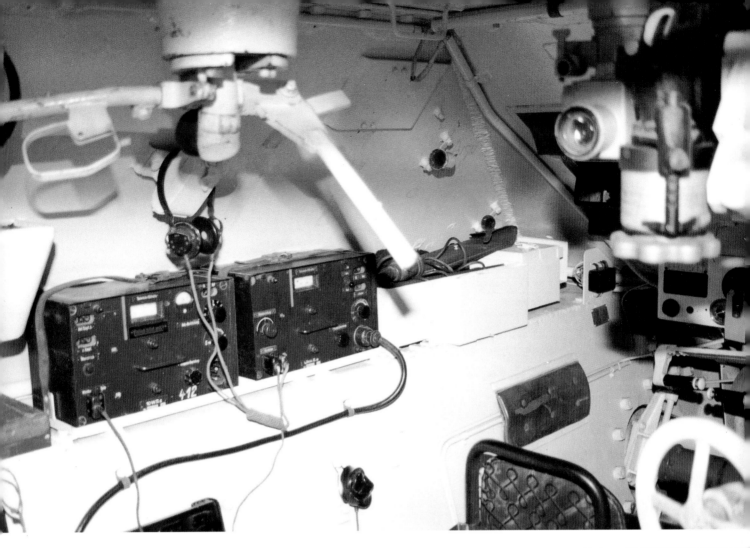

(Opposite top) This general type of mantlet, of steel cast in compound curves, was typical of several German self-propelled assault guns and tank destroyers; it was called a *saukopf* - "pig's head". The hull front armor was 60mm thick.

(Left) The 7.62mm MG34 machine gun mounted on the roof; here it has the shoulder stock fitted, but this was often omitted, as the gun could be fired, elevated and traversed by remote control from inside the fighting compartment, where a small periscope provides limited vision. Since it was fed by 50-round drums, however, it needed frequent reloading; this, and dealing with any jams, meant that the gunner or loader had to partly expose himself while he wrestled with it, his movements restricted by the small armor shields.

(Above & right) Left side of the fighting compart-ment, with driver's seat at right foreground. There are two points to note. This vehicle is one of the Hetzers taken over by the Swiss Army after the war and used until the 1960s. They kept the original German radio sets, but moved them from the rear firewall to the left sponson, as here. Above the radios, note the large control handles for the remotely operated MG34 on the roof - these were a further inconvenience for the hard-pressed loader.

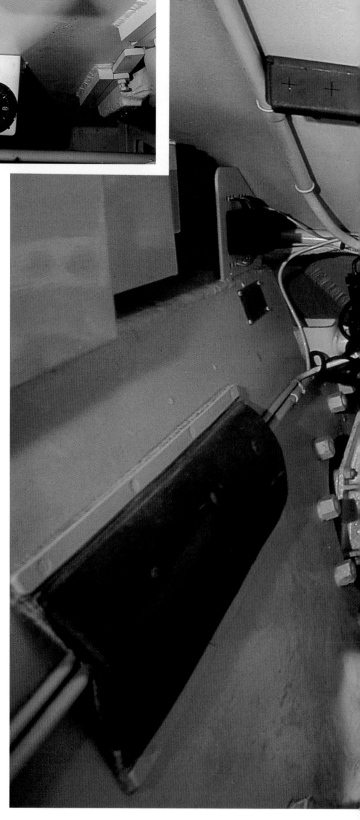

(Above & opposite) The driver's station, at front left of the hull, with the gun mount and transmission tunnel to the right. Note pads to protect the driver on the left sponson and above his head; AFV crewmen, closed down inside a vehicle with very limited vision, are in real danger of injury from being slammed around by unexpected lurches during cross-country movement. Left and below of the two vision blocks is a black box pierced for three cruciform lights; these are operated by the commander to show if he wants the driver to go left, straight ahead or right.

Hetzer Road Reports

Duane Klug: "The Hetzer is a very cramped vehicle, particularly the driver's compartment. I have a hard time getting my feet on the pedals because they are so close together. You only have two small vision ports to see out of, and you're always buttoned up; the restricted vision is the worst thing about the Hetzer. If you keep the RPM up, she'll dance right around for you, otherwise it can be quite sluggish. It has a 'pivot steer' capability that helps bring it around, and if you've got some speed up you can do a sliding turn around a corner - and that can be a little unnerving, until you learn how to compensate and control the tank. It can surprise you how responsive the Hetzer can be.

"The pre-select transmission is really great - you select the gear you want, then operate the clutch, and the gear change is made automatically, up or down. That was a tremendous advance for its time, 50 years ago."

Marc Sehring: "The Hetzer would have been a nightmare for the driver. For one thing, his visibility is very bad. You have a very narrow field of view and no sense of depth while looking through the vision blocks. It is even hard to tell if you're moving, because it is a loud vehicle with a lot of vibration, and you can creep ahead without noticing. It would be an uncomfortable tank to crew in combat, particularly for the driver, especially if you got hit; the only way out is through one hatch at the rear. Because of limited visibility, the first time you're likely to know you're in trouble is when the enemy rounds start bouncing off (or going through...) the hull. And the gunner has a very limited range of motion for the gun; the driver has to pretty much rough-aim the whole vehicle and the gunner does the fine tuning. It would be almost impossible to engage a target that was moving across your front."

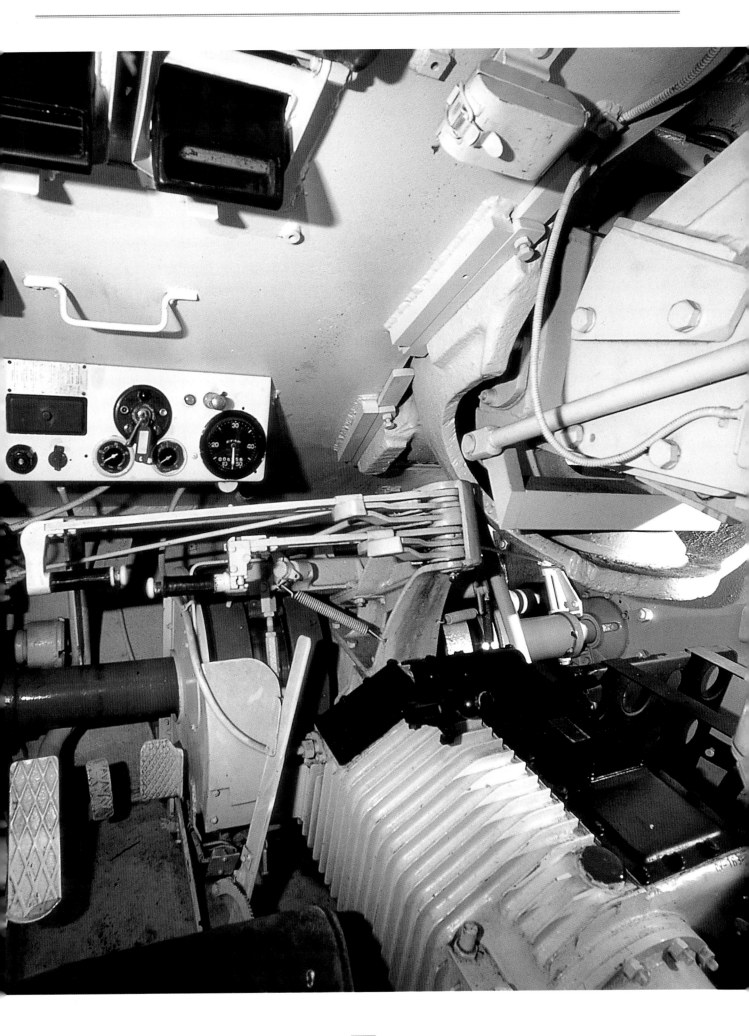

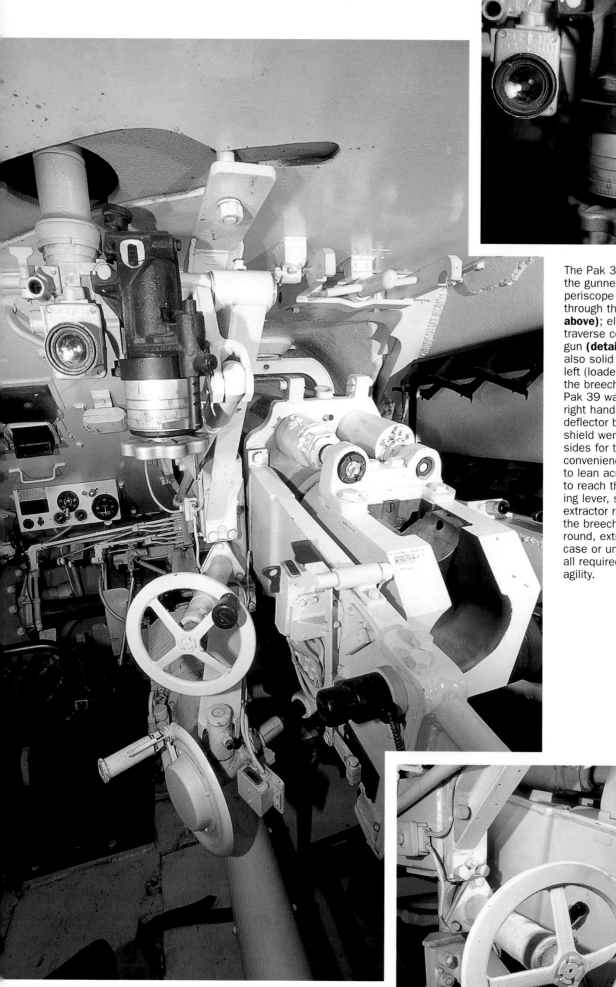

The Pak 39 gun seen from the gunner's station: note periscope sight passing up through the roof (detail, above); elevation and traverse controls on left of gun (detail, below); but also solid body shield on left (loader's) side behind the breech. Because the Pak 39 was designed for right hand operation, the deflector bar and the solid shield were on the wrong sides for the loader's convenience. He also had to lean across to the right to reach the breech operating lever, safety switch and extractor release - opening the breech for the first round, extracting a jammed case or unloading the gun all required considerable agility.

T-34/85

In any of the innumerable arguments which crop up among armor enthusiasts as to which was the best tank design of World War II, the M4 Sherman and the Panzer V Panther will always have their advocates; but for all-round performance, the author's vote for the blue ribbon has to go to the Soviet T-34. Tanks are all about firepower, protection and mobility; in its developed version the T-34 had a very powerful gun, heavy and excellently shaped armor, a first rate engine and drive train - and it simply blew the doors off the competition.

When the German Panzers first encountered properly handled T-34s in any numbers - those of Col. Mikhail Katukov's 4th Tank Brigade, at Mtsensk, south of Moscow, on 4 October 1941 - the experience was profoundly shocking. Since the launching of Operation Barbarossa in June the German tankers had been massacring their Soviet opponents in enormous numbers. Although much of the huge Red Army tank fleet was technically obsolete or mechanically unserviceable, many hundreds of excellent new KV-1 and T-34 tanks had in fact been delivered; Soviet weakness lay in the standard of command and control, communications and tactical training. Their repeated easy victories led some Panzer officers to express a puzzled contempt for their enemy that summer. Yet after Mtsensk, no less a leader than Gen. Heinz Guderian would admit the plain superiority of the T-34 over the German Panzer IV - and recommend that German designers should simply produce a direct copy of it, as the quickest solution.

Throughout the terribly costly years of 1941 and 1942, newly promoted young Russian tank officers learned and applied the hard-won lessons; and the factories - some safe far beyond the Urals, some a couple of miles from the front lines in besieged cities - kept on pouring out T-34s. The type was

steadily improved; before the appearance in early 1943 of the Panther (inspired by German study of the T-34), the Panzer divisions had nothing which could challenge it head to head. From spring 1944 the up-gunned 85mm model could give Panthers and even Tigers a run for their money - and now the balance of sheer numbers had tipped back in Russia's favour. Although newer, more powerful designs appeared by 1945, the T-34 remained by far the most numerous tank in Red Army service. It was the faithful *tridsatchetverka* ("little thirty-four") which pushed back the ramparts of Hitler's empire, all the way from Stalingrad to the streets of Berlin.

Production of the T-34/85 continued after World War II, not only in the Soviet Union but also in Poland and Czechoslovakia; one source states that it may not finally have ceased until 1964. Exact figures are unknown, but authorities estimate wartime production of all T-34 models at around 40,000, with about the same number built post-war. The T-34/85 was supplied to many foreign armies after 1945; it saw action with the North Korean, Egyptian, Syrian, Hungarian, North Vietnamese, Cuban and Angolan forces, and small numbers lingered on in Africa and Asia until the more modern T-54/T-55 series became cheaply available in the Third World. The T-34 shares with the M4 Sherman, and the British Centurion, the record for the longest service life of any AFV in history – so far...

Crewing the T-34/85

Inside, the T-34 is noticeably roomy compared to the Sherman. There is no turret basket providing a separate floor for the fighting compartment, revolving with the gun; the gunner, loader and commander sit on seats attached to the

Probably the best tank - measured against its contemporaries - of World War II: the 85mm gun version of the Russian T-34. This ex-Czechoslovak Army example is fitted out as a battalion commander's mount in 1944-45, with the turret slogan

For Stalin! In the head-on photo, note the frontal protection provided for the commander and loader when riding "head out" behind their upright hatches, and the thickness of the driver's open hatch in the glacis plate.

turret ring or to the gun, or stand on the ammunition bins which form the floor of the hull - and when the turret traverses, you'd better be ready to traverse yourself along with it, or you can get snagged in the works.

As is common in Soviet tanks, the gunner (who on earlier models of the T- 34 had to double up as the tank commander) works from the left side of the gun. The controls for the superb D-5T 85mm gun are elegantly simple: hand wheels for elevation and traverse, a single periscope for a wide field view of the area in front of the gun, and a telescopic sight for alignment with the target. The gunner uses an electric drive to traverse the turret rapidly into rough alignment with the target, then shifts to the handwheels for precision gun laying.

The TC has a flip-down seat behind the gunner, and a cupola with all-round-vision optics and a large forward-opening hatch. He operates the radio, which is mounted on the turret wall to his left. The gunner shares his hatch for entry and escape.

The loader works from the right side of the turret; it must help if he's left-handed, because serving the gun is awkward for a right-handed man. He feeds the gun initially from a ready rack holding nine rounds, stowed against the hull. Most of the ammunition - offically, another 51 rounds - is stowed in the protected bins which form the floor of the hull interior; getting it out and up to the gun, while the tank was rocking and rolling across country, must have been quite a challenge. He has his own hatch in the right side of the turret roof, but no cupola.

The driver and bow gunner sit side by side up front, with limited headroom; but because the final drive is at the rear of the tank they don't have a big transmission tunnel filling up their space. The driver uses a conventional pair of track

Continued on page 86

(Left) Note rough finish of turret casting: in World War II all that mattered was getting tanks out of the factory, onto the flatcar, and off to the front.

(Right) Engine compartment and final drive; the rear hull plate protecting the 500hp V-12 diesel was 45mm thick, as was the armor over the interior fuel tanks dispersed around the sides. The engine bulkhead was thin, making the fighting compartment very noisy.

(Left) Extra fuel tanks strapped round the outside of the engine compartment have long been a feature of Russian tanks; the theory is that if they are going to get hit and burn, it would be best if they burned outside the tank. In fact, being diesel- rather than petrol-fuelled, and with most of its ammunition stored so low down, the T-34 did not burn as readily as German tanks.

(Left) The glacis, 47mm thick and sloped at a dramatic 60 degrees to throw off shot, was a great step forward in protection. Note the hammerhead tow hooks each side of the spare track plates; the bow gun's protective mantlet and telescope port; and the two driver's hatch periscopes.

   (Right) Paired, rubbertyred, full height, independently sprung steel roadwheels of the Christie-type suspension, with 19in-wide tracks, gave a rollercoaster ride but excellent floatation.

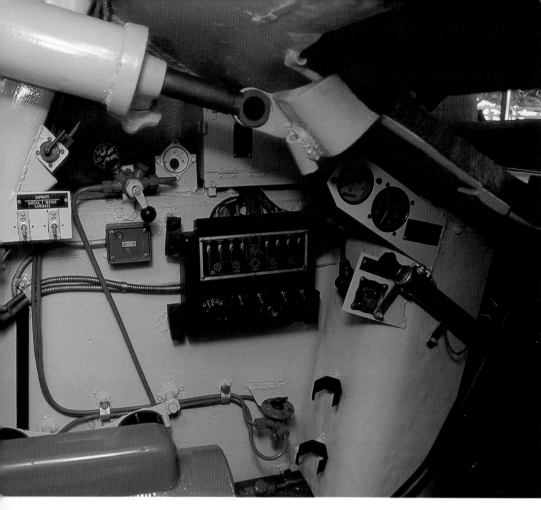

(Left) The left side of the driver's station: at top left, the cylinder of the front hatch counterweight assembly; bottom left, compressed air cylinder for cold weather starter; on small panel left of hatch, tachometer and speedometer.

(Right) The front hull, looking forwards into the driver's and bow gunner's stations from low down in the loader's station inside the turret ring. The driver's steering levers, pedals and gear shift are quite evident; the machine gun has a canvas bag rigged to catch empties, and plentiful spare drums stowed around it - note also its telescopic "peep". An escape hatch is let into the floor in front of the gunner's seat.

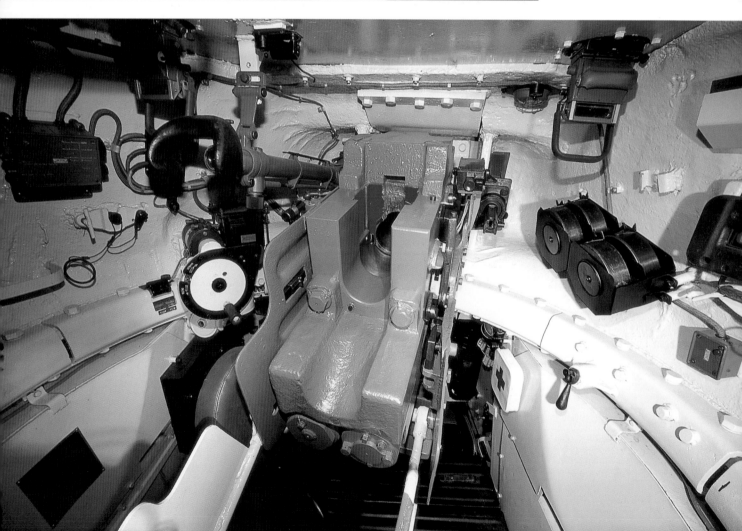

(Left) Looking forward from the loader's station right of the gun breech: note the floor made up of ammunition bins; drum magazine rack for co-axial machine gun on right of turret; below it, turret traverse lock. This turret has been called cramped; but it appears fairly roomy compared with the M4A1 Sherman, and positively luxurious after the badly designed two-man turret of the old T-34/76.

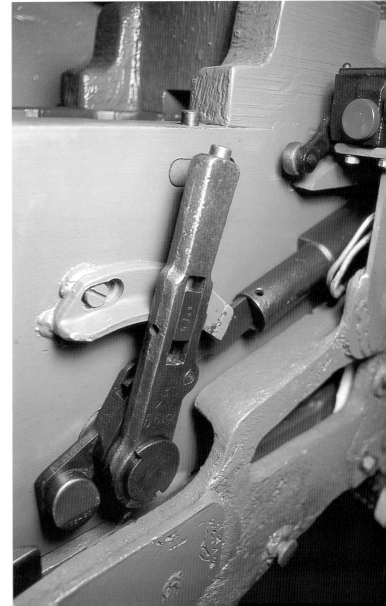

(Right) The right side of the breech of the D-5T 85mm gun, with the lever used to crank open the breech before loading the first round - recoil opens it thereafter - and the gun safety switch, top right.

(Top & above) Left side of the breech, from behind the gunner's station: note brown gunner's seat flipped up; periscope and telescopic primary sight above elevation and traverse controls; gun control switch boxes on turret wall.

This gun could penetrate the side or rear armour of a PzKw VI Tiger at a mile, but its turret and hull front armor only at about 200 yards. The Tiger could punch an 88mm AP round through the T-34/85's turret front at 1,400 yards, but had to come to within 100 yards to be sure of penetrating the glacis. In battle, tactical skill and fast, accurate shooting counted for more than cold mathematics. In August 1944, in the first encounter with King Tigers on the Russian Front, a heavily camouflaged T-34/85 ambushed and knocked out two in as many minutes from 200 yards broadside on, using four special high velocity tungsten-cored AP rounds on each. He then got a third with a single round through the rear plate.

braking levers for steering control, just as in most other tanks of the period. These are notoriously stiff, and cross-country navigation requires considerable brute strength; it is a long-standing joke that T-34 drivers must have been recruited (or deliberately bred...) about five feet tall, with ape-like arms of roughly the same length. Stirrup-type pedals are provided for the clutch (left) and parking brake (right), and a pedal operates the foot throttle (far right); the hand throttle and gear shift lever are to the driver's right. An extremely Spartan array of instruments to the driver's left and front report on basic engine conditions. A high pressure compressed air tank is attached in front of or left of the driver, part of an ingenious and very efficient system for starting the engine in cold weather; the primary starter motor is electrical.

When out of battle the driver enjoys much better forward vision (and ventilation) than most of his contemporaries: a hatch large enough for him to enter and leave the tank is set in the glacis ahead of his station, and can be hinged up and fixed open when conditions allow. When it is locked down for combat forward vision is as mediocre as in other tanks of the time, through two periscopes set in the hatch.

In early model T-34s the bow gunner/radio operator often didn't have much to do, since only the tanks of platoon commanders and above were even fitted with radios - the rest had to communicate by waving signal flags.... In the T-34/85, which saw the radio moved up into the new three-man turret, he was still not over-employed unless the driver got killed or wounded, when he was supposed to drag him out of the seat and take over.

His ball-mounted 7.62mm DT machine gun was aimed (in a rudimentary fashion) through a small x2 telescopic sight; it was useful against any infantry foolish enough to position themselves directly in front of the hull. The DT is fed by drum magazines, and a plentiful supply of spare drums are provided in racks to the bow gunner's front and right. The gun has a telescoping shoulder stock and a separately stowed bipod mount; it was the bow gunner's job to dismount it for ground combat if the crew abandoned the tank. He had plenty of time: unless by some miracle the floor hatch had enough ground clearance, he wasn't going anywhere until either the driver or the loader had made it out of their own hatches.

(Left) The radio equipment in this ex-Czech Army tank is of Czechoslovak manufacture, but installed in the original position high on the left turret wall, convenient to the commander's hand. Two of the cupola vision blocks are seen above it.

(Below) A slightly confusing angle, but a useful shot to help "tie up" the various components in the left side of the turret. We are looking upwards from the floor of the gunner's station, past the gunlaying controls and telescope sight at left and center, to the radio at upper left, and the inside of the commander's cupola and hatch at top center.

T-34 Road Report

Marc Sehring: "The T-34 is crude, basic, noisy, smoky, smelly - a very charming, very Russian tank! I like the T-34; it is simple, without frills, designed to fight and survive, without any consideration for crew comfort. Working in the turret could be dangerous. Visibility isn't great, particularly for the bow gunner, who can't see anything unless it's directly in front of his little 'scope. But it will take off and run really well - it is a fast, reliable tank.

"The driver has to be built like a horse to drive it, but once you're out in open country it rides very well; the tracks are wide enough to give it good floatation. You are surrounded by fuel and ammunition, but the armor is thick and beautifully shaped - the shape of the vehicle was well ahead of its time.

"The V-12 engine is a great powerplant, very well designed and highly dependable. I've never had a problem with Soviet engines, anyway. They do burn oil, but the Russians planned for that, and you've got a big tank to keep the crankcase filled - if you aren't burning oil in a T-34, it means there's no oil in the engine. And the air start system works really well - the engine fires up every time.

"The gunner's sight is pretty good for its time - good field of view and a pretty bright sight system. The turret traverse system is simple but effective. The real problem is communication between the commander and the gunner, which has to be good, because the gunner doesn't have a wide field of view.

"You can't really sneak up on somebody with them, but they weren't designed for that - they were designed for the attack. And if they'd gone up against our American tanks of the time, we'd have lost: it's a much better design than the M4 Sherman, with a lower silhouette, much better gun, better armor, better slope, a great suspension system, simpler, easier to maintain - a superior machine."

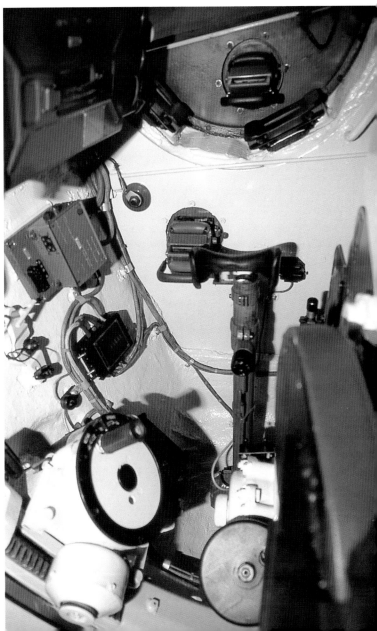

Chapter 3

Wars Warm and Cold

M37 Howitzer Motor Carriage

The development of armored divisions before and during World War II was not just a story of bigger, faster, better protected tanks. Tanks which advance alone are vulnerable to a range of enemy weapons, from dug-in long range anti-tank guns to courageous infantrymen with hand-held bazookas or shaped charges. The effective armored formation must include infantry, as mobile across country as the tanks, and with some measure of armor protection to allow them to ride quickly into the forward edge of battle - thus the halftracks of World War II, and today's fully tracked, fully armored personnel carriers and infantry fighting vehicles. Tanks and infantry also need their own artillery support, capable of accompanying them across any terrain, to provide heavy howitzer barrages onto area targets.

All the major combatants of World War II fielded "self-propelled artillery" in the shape of howitzers mounted in partly enclosed, thinly armored housings on tracked chassis; and it was obviously economic to use the chassis and running gear of existing tanks - sometimes their own current battle tanks, sometimes captured or obsolete types. The best known Allied SP gun was the 105mm howitzer mounted on the M4 Sherman chassis - the M7 Priest. At the end of the war a new light tank, the M24 Chaffee, began to replace the M5 Stuart in the recon role. This had a well-designed and well-powered chassis and suspension, which were later used as the basis for a number of other armored fighting vehicles. One of them was the M37 Howitzer Motor Carriage, of which a splendidly restored and stowed example is illustrated here.

(**Above**) The tall machine gun "pulpit" off-set beside the gun gives this HMC an immediate look of the old World War II M7 Priest, but a glance at the running gear quickly identifies it as based on the M24 Chaffee. The 16in-wide tracks and 20.5 ton loaded weight give a reasonably low ground pressure of 11.7 pounds. The M24 also served as the basis for the M19 twin-40mm anti-aircraft GMC, and the heavy M41 155mm HMC. Only about 300 of these M37s were built from 1945, but - like the M19 and M41 - it did see combat in the Korean War, with such units as the 58th Field Artillery Battalion (which fought with the 3rd Infantry Division).

The open box body characteristic of SP guns of this vintage gave some protection against small arms and shell splinters, but no overhead cover; they were not intended to fight in the front line of battle, delivering direct fire, but to lob shells over hills from the rear gun lines. Aircraft were also getting too fast to track with hand-aimed guns; and that .50cal pulpit was as much for psychological comfort as in any serious expectation that the crew would have to use it for real.

(**Right**) The driver's station at left front of the M37 is identical to that of the M24 tank, though the latter also had an assistant driver/bow gunner's position with duplicated controls. The simple panel houses dual instruments for the two 110hp Cadillac V-8 petrol engines.

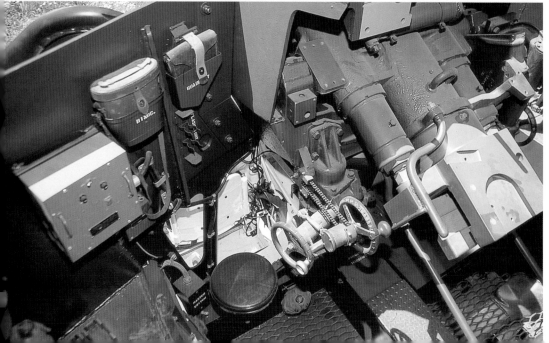

(**Above & left**) Breech area, looking forward: like many pre-existing guns pressed into service in AFVs, rather than being designed for the job from scratch, the howitzer has been turned on its side to make it fit. The box body gives the seven-man crew more room to stow their gear than tankers enjoy; everything has its place, from the striped aiming stakes to binoculars and canteens. Note the crew's .30cal carbines stowed with a fuel can and six "ready rounds" on the right of the breech.

(**Below**) At the right front of the hull six fused rounds are clipped in a ready rack, for a "hip shoot" or emergency fire mission. The rest of the main gun ammo - officially listed as 26 rounds, but photos show twice that many carried - were kept in their protective fiberboard packing tubes and stacked upright in bins along the hull sides.

T-55

The Soviet T-54/T-55 series is the hands-down, all-time most popular tank in history. Perhaps 100,000 examples have been built; and these tanks have served with no less than 50 armies and quasi-armies throughout Eastern Europe, the Middle East, Africa, Asia and South America. The T-54 was developed immediately after World War II; the first prototype appeared in 1946, and it went into Red Army service by 1950. The very similar but improved T-55 followed in 1960. The USSR supplied and licensed them at favourable terms to its satellites, and to other favored clients as part of its drive for world-wide influence throughout the Cold War. The series was adaptable; improvements were steadily incorporated, and many specialist modifications and conversions were carried out over the years. Russia was still building T-55s in 1979; and they are readily available today for about $10,000 US per copy.

The T-54/T-55 family have seen combat on many battlefields, but will forever be associated with the Middle East wars of 1967 and 1973. In the Sinai desert in 1967 the Egyptian Army lost nearly 400 to Israeli aircraft and in battle with Israeli M48 Pattons and Centurions. In October 1973, after a much more evenly balanced start, enough were captured for Israel to take them into service, with suitable modifications - a considerable compliment. In the savage tank battles on the Golan Heights in 1973 Syrian tankers very nearly broke through Israel's defensive line.

Several hundred Indian Army T-54s and T-55s also saw action against Pakistan in December 1971 - interestingly, coming up against Pakistan's T-59s, the Chinese-built version, in the Chaamb sector. Honours were roughly even, despite the Indians having the advantage of better AP ammunition and infrared night fighting systems. These active IR systems, fitted to the T-55 since the late 1950s, were useful back then, but are a real hazard on the modern battlefield. One IR searchlight is slaved to the main gun, and a smaller one is installed on the TC's cupola (see photos), allowing him to search for and acquire targets. IR radiation is invisible to the unaided eye, but highly visible to anybody on the battlefield with a similar system; a tank which powers up an IR searchlight is essentially shouting "Over here, guys!" to any enemy tank with an IR viewer within line-of-sight. Modern passive night vision systems have entirely outclassed IR nowadays.

More than 3,500 T-54s and T-55s made up the bulk of Saddam Hussein's Iraqi armored force during the 1990/91 Gulf War; huge numbers of these were destroyed by US aircraft and later Coalition ground attacks. While the T-55 was a great tank in its day, that day has passed; it is totally outclassed by tanks like the M1 Abrams - whose fire control systems can easily home in on it in any light conditions; whose gun can easily outrange and penetrate it; whose armor is virtually impervious to its AP rounds; and which can outmanoeuver it on any battlefield.

(Previous pages & above right) T-55A in Czech Army markings; this variant - lacking the bow machine gun - appeared in 1963. Fully combat loaded, these tanks weigh about 40 tons and exert about 11.5psi ground pressure. The series typically uses a 250hp model V-54 diesel engine, a massive air-cooled V-12; the T-55 has a slightly up-rated model V-55. Top road speed is about 30mph, and combat range about 250 miles.

T-55 Road Report

Marc Sehring: "I am really impressed with the way the Soviets put these vehicles together: they're monsters, they're crude, they have lots of horsepower, lots of armor, a really big gun, lots of ammunition, lots of fuel, and the engine just drinks oil - this is a man's tank!

"I love to drive the T-55; it is an awesome machine. That big V-12 diesel sounds just amazing, with a tremendous roar and a distinctive clinking from the track linkage. They steer very well, much better than American tanks of the same period. The night vision system, smoke capability, and the deep fording capability all made the tank really capable for its day. In fact, it has lots of little bells and whistles: compass, excellent compressed air or electric starters, lots of back-up systems - you can even clean the periscopes with air pressure, from inside. The 100mm gun was excellent for its day, and you've got pretty good vision, even buttoned up.

"It is harder to maintain; the access to the engine is somewhat limited, although the filters can all be cleaned in the field. It is designed to be maintained in the field, and it has enough back-up systems that you can overcome most failures. The components are beefy, particularly compared to American equipment. It is a very robust tank, and hard to break; that means that in combat you can worry about the enemy rather than your own vehicle."

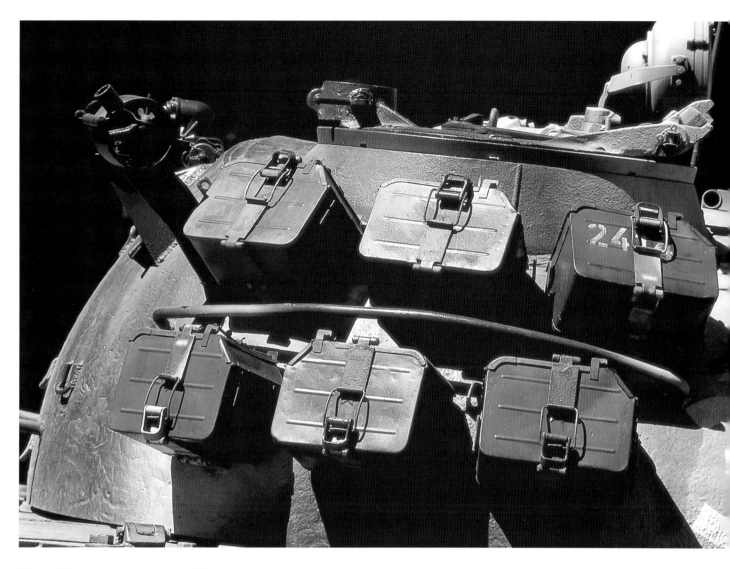

(Above) The turret is a massive casting with a welded-on armor plate roof. At first the T-55 was not fitted with the external 12.7mm DShK heavy anti-aircraft machine gun; in the late 1960s, with the growth of NATO's tactical ground attack fleet, they were retro-issued, and the ammo had to be stored in these external boxes.

(Right) The very sharply sloped glacis is nearly seven inches thick; the straight weld distinguishes the T-55 from the T-54.

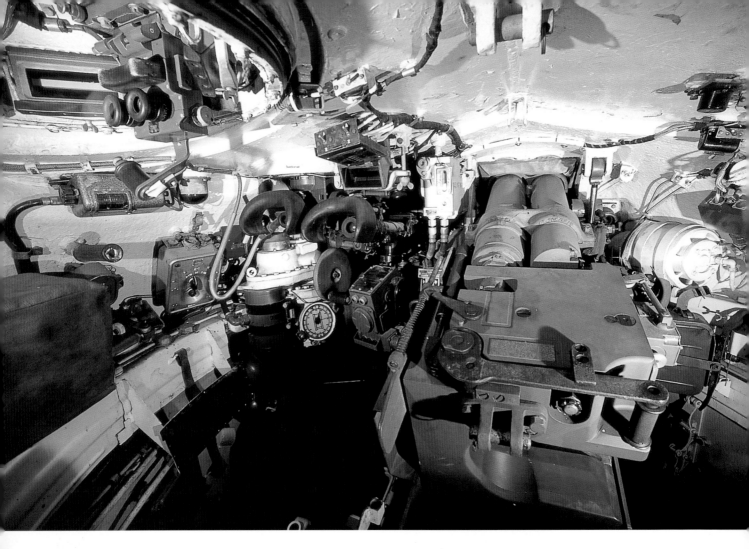

(Left) Looking from gunner's station to right rear of the turret, under the loader's hatch; the AK is jammed behind a clip for 100mm ammo. The turret looks deceptively roomy - it is in fact very cramped, especially when the (still inadequate) load of 43 x 100mm rounds are stowed.

(Right) Driver's station at front left: controls are conventional - brake, clutch and accelerator pedals, lateral steering levers, and a five-speed gear shift. He can drive "head out", but the gun cannot traverse if he does. The driver is not separated from the fighting compartment by a bulk-head; the whole T-55A inte-rior has an overpressure system, to keep contaminated air out in a nuclear/biological/chemical environment. Diesel fuel and main gun ammo are stowed to the right of the driver's compartment.

(Left & right) Commander's and gunner's stations on left of D-10T2S 100mm gun breech; and detail of gun and turret controls and telescopic sights. The gun is stabilized in both axes, and has power elevation; traverse is electrical with manual back-up - about 30 per cent slower than Western hydraulics. The TC acquires a target with his designator sight, traverses the turret into a rough aim, passes estimated range to the gunner, and orders the loader to select a round; the gunner then takes final aim, and the TC gives the order to fire. The small turret size, and his awkard position right of the gun, hamper the loader wrestling with the 50-pound shells - rate of fire is typically only half as fast as with NATO tanks.

M60 Patton

It is a reflection on the extraordinary speed with which we adapt to new circumstances that it is already quite hard to remember the atmosphere of the 1970s and 1980s, when the prospect of all-out war between the forces of the Warsaw Pact and NATO seemed very real. The M60 - which kept the name Patton, first used for the M46 tank of the 1950s - was designed and built to fight that war which never came. Introduced in 1960 in direct response to the appearance of the Russian T-54 series, this 45-tonner retained a few features of the earlier M48 but was armed with a deadly new 105mm gun, and powered by a safe and frugal 750hp diesel giving a 300-mile combat range.

The M60A1, with an improved turret, appeared in 1962; it served with the US Army and Marine Corps throughout the 1960s and 1970s, its engine, electrical systems, and fire control equipment being steadily up-graded. Only engineer and bridge-laying variants saw action in Vietnam; but gun tanks saw hard and costly fighting in the ranks of the Israeli armored brigades in the 1973 Middle East war and the Lebanon invasion of 1982. This battle experience identified several weak points, leading to improved protection of the turret ring area; the replacement of the very inflammable hydraulic fluid used in the traverse system; and the attachment of "reactive" explosive slabs outside the turret, to detonate HEAT projectiles before they touched the steel.

The final M60A3 version appeared at the end of the 1970s, incorporating all the successive improvements. Intended to face any Warsaw Pact onslaught in Central Europe, it was designed and equipped to destroy T-55s, T-62s and APCs by the platoon and the company, and to go head-to-head with its natural foe, the T-72. It might have succeeded, too: the M60A3 is a superb tank, with a better gun system than the first generation M1 Abrams. Though it is less heavily armored than the T-64 and T-72, its dual-stabilized 105mm gun - based on the British L7 series - has a hyper- velocity AP round with a depleted uranium core which can punch through any Soviet armor at long range. The US Army rates its effective reach at 3,000 yards, about 30 per cent better than current Soviet equivalents; and despite the M60's taller profile, the ability to depress the gun to -10 degrees allows it to engage from a lower hull-down position.

The M60 is powered by a big 12-cylinder diesel coupled to an excellent automatic transmission. People who have driven a variety of tanks acclaim the M60 as one of the very easiest, and it is used for driver training at the Patton Museum at Fort Knox, Kentucky. It is set up very much like a conventional automobile with automatic transmission, with just two forward gears and one reverse - a considerable improvement over the manual shifting required in earlier US tanks and current Russian models. Six paired road wheels, torsion bar suspension, and massive tracks give the tank a very comfortable ride across difficult terrain, and excellent traction on the slimy German hillsides it had to negotiate in the annual NATO "Reforger" exercises of the 1980s. The M60 will do 30mph on a good road, less on broken ground - but it will still be pretty fast. It will get across an eight-foot ditch and climb a 60 degree gradient; you can ford a stream four feet deep without preparation, or 13 feet deep with the snorkel.

One strikingly different variant, the M60A2 (unofficially nicknamed the "Starship" by crews frustrated at its complexity), entered limited US Army service in the middle 1970s. It featured a new, smaller turret mounting the same M162 dual purpose 152mm gun/Shillelagh missile launcher as installed on the M551 Sheridan. With two-axis stabilization for both the main gun and the cupola, and a laser rangefinder (a US first), the TC could designate and lock onto a target for automatic "hand-off" while the gunner engaged another target. Unfortunately the M60A2 suffered most of the same problems with the missile and the fragile, damp-prone, unreliably "self-consuming" combustible case ammunition as did the Sheridan; and while these were eventually sorted out, by that time advances in conventional gun ammunition and fire control systems cut its career short.

(Opposite top) A platoon of M60A3 tanks rumbles towards the sound of guns at the massive US Marine Corps training area around Twentynine Palms in California's Mojave Desert. They are fitted with clusters of smoke grenade dischargers on the turret; and - see the orange "bubblegum" light rising from the rear - with the MILES laser system which accurately monitors "hits" during training battles.

(Above) An M60A1 out to pasture; apart from the absence of the smoke grenade tubes this example is structurally complete.

(Right) This shot reminds us of the abuse that tank tracks have to endure, particularly from abrasive sand and gravel; even today's massively strong steel and rubber components don't last for ever, and track life is an important factor in the calculation of a unit's overall combat readiness.

(Above) The turret bustle rack provides handy external stowage for such necessities as water, spare track pads, machine gun ammunition, tarpaulins, cases of MRE rations, and the crew's packs and bedrolls. The insignia board shows the tank's position in the unit in coded form: the shapes of the yellow background and central OD patch indicate the battalion within the brigade, and the company within the battalion; the white III identifies 3rd Platoon, and the single bar below it the first tank in the platoon.

(Right) An M60A1 driver peers up from his solitary station centered in the front of the hull - note the swivelling hatch.

(Right) M60A1: this powerful xenon searchlight, slaved to the main gun, was a feature of the M60, A1 and A2 variants.

(Below) The enclosed, independently traversing commander's cupola mounting a .50cal machine gun was a development of one fitted on the earlier M48A2. It proved unpopular with Israeli combat crews; in its high position it was sometimes hit by tank shells, which ripped the whole ton-weight assembly out, and the IDF later replaced it with a lower, conventional cupola designed to protect a "head out" commander from above. Before the development of laser rangefinders, coincidence optical systems were the norm; the TC's periscope and rangefinder were positioned centrally on the cupola, and the lateral optics as far apart as possible - see inset, the protruding ball housing of the left optic.

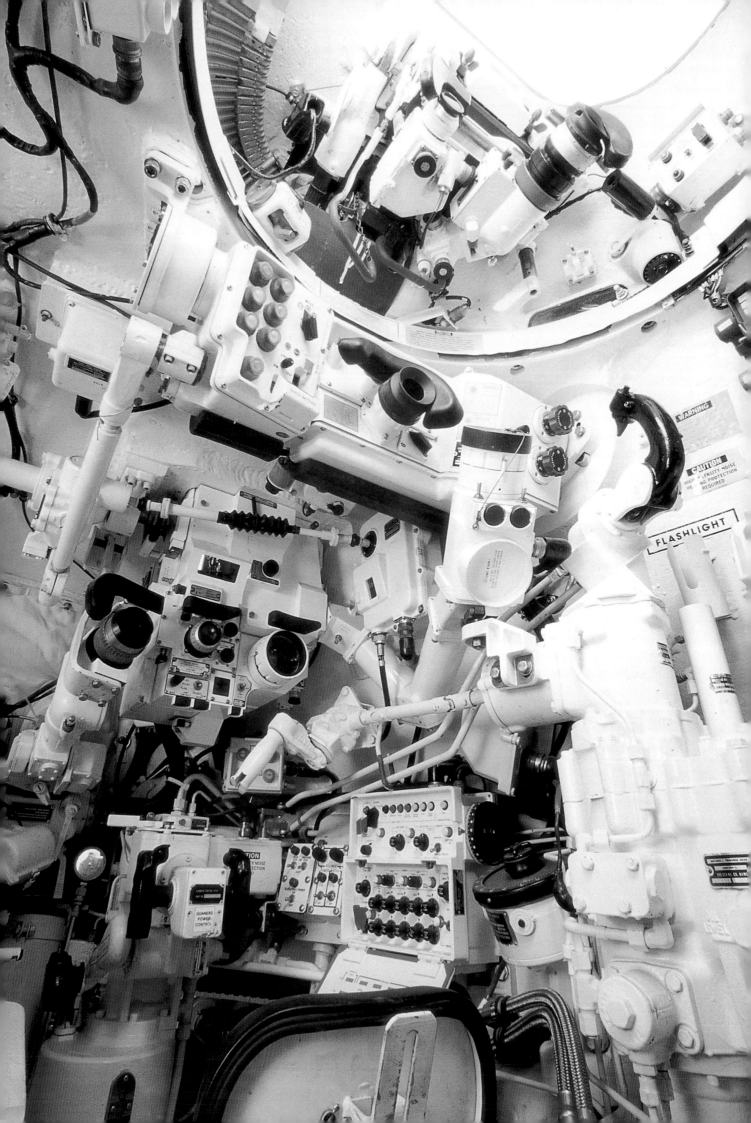

(Opposite & above)
Gunner's and commander's stations, M60A3: the proliferation of "black boxes" in a modern tank reflects the enormous advances in target acquisition and fire control in the past 20 years, due to such new technologies as computer science and lasers.

In World War II a tank gunner looked for an enemy tank through a telescopic sight; lined it up with the sight reticle; made an educated guess at range depending on how big he thought it was and how much of the sight picture it filled; "layed off" deflection for angle and speed of motion based on his eyesight and practical experience - and fired, hoping to correct his aim by observing the fall of shot.

The M60A3 was introduced in 1978 with a laser rangefinder and a solid state ballistic fire control computer; a laser beam is "bounced" off the target, feeding the computer with exact range data. It was soon fitted with a thermal sight; this "sees" and distinguishes between the natural infrared emissions which all objects give off, and amplifies those of e.g. a warm-engined vehicle into a sight picture - not only at night, but also through fog, rain, and the dust and smoke of battle. The M60A3 was the first tank fitted with this device, which greatly increases the chances of a first-round kill. It also has a sensor which feeds the computer directly with wind speed information, taking into account the type of round selected while correcting the aim automatically.

(Right) Gunner's fire control computer input panel.

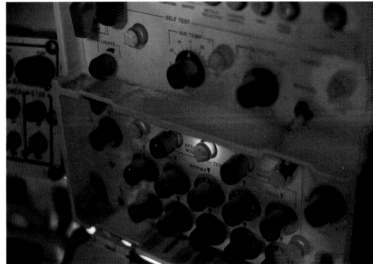

M60A3 Road Report

Richard Boyd: "The A3 is clearly not a modern tank anymore. Its armor protection is nowhere near that of current tanks, and its 105mm gun is no longer equal to the most modern tank guns - although it would still be formidable under some conditions. The A3 was excellent in its day, with the best thermal sights ever manufactured - better than the first generation sights in the original M1 Abrams. It had a very good fire control system that required a well-trained crew - not as 'idiot-friendly' as the M1 fire control, but devastating in the hands of a sharp crew. I went to gunneries where we never shot twice at the same target, and never missed one. The results of tank combat during the Gulf War showed that with American training and fire control systems the probability of getting first-round kills on anything out to 2,500 or 3,000 meters is very high.

"The M60A3 was not as mobile a tank as the current generation, although it was good in its day. It was a very easy tank to learn to drive, at least at the entry level - it only took about ten seconds to teach somebody all they needed to know (in theory) to drive one. You have a T-bar for steering, a brake, a gear selector with just two positions for forward motion, and a starter button. You get in the tank, push the starter button, put the tank in gear, pressed the accelerator, and away you go - it really is pretty much dummy-proof."

(Above & right) Radio installation and some of the ready ammunition stowage in an M60A1 turret bustle. These protective tubes for individual 105mm rounds are fitted wherever there is room for them, including 26 flanking the seat in the driver's compartment; in all 63 rounds are carried for the main gun, plus 900 for the .50cal machine gun in the TC's cupola, and another 5,950 for the 7.62mm co-axial gun. The turret is spacious and well laid out, with room for even tall crewmen to stand up comfortably; its format is conventional, with the loader on the left of the gun beneath his own roof hatch, and the gunner sitting ahead of the TC's knees on the right.

M551 Sheridan

Under the urgent conditions of a shooting war it is inevitable that new equipment - aircraft, guns, tanks - will be sent into the line prematurely, before they have been thoroughly tested. Their equally inevitable shortcomings will show up in combat, rather than in the controlled privacy of a test program; and inevitably, men will die before the problems are identified and solved. Under the pressure of war, with line commanders crying out for new weapons to reverse an enemy advantage, all this is unavoidable; sometimes, however, it is the unnecessary result of simple bureaucratic bungling.

Like so many other revolutionary designs, the M551 Sheridan airborne reconnaissance tank seemed like a good idea at the time. It was a response to conflicting demands: for a fast, agile recon tank light enough to be air- dropped with the airborne division, but heavily armed enough to give the paratroopers some serious anti-tank muscle. The first requirement worked out pretty well: the Sheridan is fast, manoeuvrable, and genuinely air-droppable. Once on the ground and reunited with its separately parachuted crew, the M551 is a first rate AFV for the recon and cavalry missions, able to shoot, scoot, and communicate. Its armor is far too light to survive a head-to-head with an enemy Main Battle Tank, but that isn't its job.

The problems arose from the ambitious, exotic armament. Since 1959 designers had been studying the concept which emerged as the MGM-57 Shillelagh missile launcher/152mm gun system, for use in various planned new tanks both light and medium. A guided missile would give excellent anti-tank performance without the massive recoil of a big cannon, and could thus be fired from a light vehicle. To keep costs down, the other types of ammo needed would be fired from the same weapon as more conventional shells. But for various reasons it was also decided to develop "self-consuming" or combustible projectile cases for these - cases made of material which, apart from a small metal endpiece, would burn away to nothing in the barrel at the moment of firing.

Development of the tank itself went smoothly; but the armament caused one headache after another throughout the 1960s. The missile initially had a bad habit of squirting out of the end of the tube only to collapse to the ground, where it flopped around in front of the tank. The early version of the gun and ammunition system proved more hazardous to its crews than to any enemy; trials reports made hair-raising reading - tales of burning debris in the breech and turret, and crews passing out from the fumes - and major redesign work had to be carried out under great pressure of time.

To head off growing criticism from Congress and the Army of this slow and increasingly costly project, the developing agencies were anxious to show off the M551 in action in Vietnam. There was no need for its anti-tank missile out there; and although it certainly offered the Armored Cavalry recon units much greater punch than the light weapons which they were rigging to their ACAV personnel carriers, the haste with which the bureaucrats insisted on bundling it off to the Asian battlefield invited serious criticism. The combustible case ammo was still dogged by serious problems when the first Sheridans were shipped out in January 1969, to fight in the ranks of the 1/11th and 3/4th Armored Cavalry.

The 1/11th, who traded in M113 ACAVs for the Sheridan, approved of the increased firepower of its big HE shell, and its spectacularly effective "Beehive" flechette round (which fired nearly 10,000 small steel darts). The 3/4th, who exchanged tough M48A2 tanks for the new design, were a lot less enthusiastic; and reports of the M551's shortcomings became something of a scandal.

The force of the recoil when it fired (which wasn't every time - the firing circuit was balky) lifted the front of the M551 a foot and a half off the ground, and threw the crew around so badly that they had to hold on tight to keep from being injured. *Duane Klug* recalls: "The concussion from the 152mm gun is just tremendous. For the TC, standing in the turret, it is like getting hit hard in the face. Inside the turret you've got the 'idiot handles' to grab, but you still get slammed around really badly. Firing that thing is an absolutely unreal experience." More seriously, the shock also disrupted the turret's notoriously unreliable electrical systems, and sometimes ruptured the recoil system.

The combustible case ammo was dangerously fragile, coming apart under any sort of shock or rough handling; and was prone to spoilage in the damp tropical climate. When in February 1969 a 3/4th tank triggered a mine - which would have done only minor wheel damage to an M48 - the blast detonated the stowed ammo, killing the driver and destroying the Sheridan. Minor battle impacts, damp, and even fast driving across rough terrain caused distortion of the caseless rounds, which then refused to feed.

The aluminum armor was extremely vulnerable to mines. Although extra titanium plates were later added, the M551's poor "survivability" against mines and RPGs always preyed on the minds of its crews; Vietnam photos frequently show all but the driver riding outside for a quick getaway, and they were often too nervous of the volatile ammunition exploding to carry a realistic combat load. Once damaged, the M551 - already terribly costly - was often unrepairable. Finally, the 300hp V-6 water-cooled, turbocharged diesel engine frequently failed due to overheating.

Vietnam was probably the last place on earth the Sheridan should have been sent: a battlefield which exaggerated its weaknesses, and where its main strength - heavy anti-tank firepower - was irrelevant. Nevertheless, by the time production ceased (after about 1,700 vehicles) in 1970, some 200 were in Vietnam, serving with most US Cavalry units. By the time the last were pulled out in late 1971 more than 100 had been destroyed or written off.

*   *   *

The Sheridan's problems were gradually resolved in piecemeal fashion by retro-fits and component modifications; and the M551A ultimately became a workhorse for the Cav during the 1970s, despite persistent maintenance problems

Continued on page 110

(Previous page) Profile of the M551. The hull is of welded aluminum armor, the turret of welded steel; it has torsion bar suspension, and rear sprocket drive.

(Below) On the road again, an ex-82nd Airborne Sheridan painted up in the markings of 3/73rd Armor noses down a woodland trail. The M551 has very good mobiity; with a top speed of about 43mph, it can turn on a dime, and at under 16 tons weight it has excellent floatation. Note the driver's hatch, with three periscopes - the middle one can take an infrared lens for night driving.

(Opposite) The shallow, sharply sloped turret of the M551, covered with optics and smoke grenade dischargers, stowed MG ammo boxes, jerrycans

and tarp rolls. The cupola, with ten vision blocks giving all- round views, is retro-fitted with an armored "crow's nest" to protect the commander when he is manning the .50cal machine gun; this will stop small arms fire, but no part of the Sheridan is proof against anything heavier than .50cal bursts. Even an RPG is guaranteed to make a mess of it, and the M551 relies on speed, agility, and concealment to stay out of trouble. The big low-light telescope mounted above the machine gun allows accurate fire on infantry, softskin vehicles or other point targets out to ranges of 2km (1.25 miles), in full auto or single shots. Another 7.62mm gun is mounted co- axially with the 152mm tube. Note also the open driver's hatch, rotated up and back into the hull.

M551 Sheridan Road Report

Lt.Col.Charles Donnell commanded 3rd Battalion, 73rd Armor, 82nd Airborne Division during Operation Desert Storm: "The Sheridan is a kind of maintenance nightmare. It was very advanced for its time, but the electronics were outdated when we used it in the desert. The circuit cards shake loose and terminals corrode in ways that don't happen with the Abrams and Bradley. The engine installation made maintenance more difficult than it needed to be, and we had recurring problems with the torque converter...[This] incorporates a flywheel which, when over-torqued, will break and protect the engine or transmission from more serious damage - but when it breaks, you're out of action just the same! And that caseless ammunition is stacked every-where in the turret - a real hazard if you get hit with an HE round or even explode a mine.

"But having said all that, the tank was perfect for its role. It has a huge gun, and a very effective missile. The armor is proof against 12.7mm heavy machine gun fire even at point blank range over most of the hull. You've got two very good machine guns with the latest up-grade, and the 152mm canister round was just awesome. If you air-drop a Sheridan into an airhead, you give the enemy some serious problems right away. We worked out some good strategies to do that, including putting the crew on the same aircraft and having them follow the tank out on the same pass over the drop zone...the crew would land close to the tank and could de-rig it and get it into action fast.

"Despite what you hear about the main gun, firing it was kind of fun, even if it seemed a bit like a religious experience some-times. The front three road wheels come off the ground when it fires, and the front of the vehicle lifts a couple of feet in the air.

"It drives well, and will go over just about anything. It is very good in soft soil and is very manoeuvrable. The short gun tube allows you to manoeuver in amongst trees where a larger tank couldn't fit. It isn't as fast as the M1, but it is a very agile tank. And the Sheridan has a very low profile that lets you tuck it into the landscape: if it is in hull-defilade position, it can just about disappear at 500 or 600 meters."

WARNING
DO NOT LOOK DIRECTLY INTO THE SOURCE IN INFRARED
HEADLIGHTS WHEN SERVICE EYE DAMAGE CAN RESULT

INSTALLATION INSTRUCTIONS

(Above left & left) Left and right of the gun tube, as viewed, are the ports through the mantlet for the gunner's M129 telescopic sight and the co-ax machine gun. The box immediately above the tube houses the MGM-57 Shillelagh missile guidance system; when in use its armored flap is dropped to expose the optics. The Shillelagh is followed in flight by the gunner, who keeps the target aligned with the sight reticle; this automatically sends guidance corrections to an infrared tracker in the tail of the missile. It takes an appreciable time for the gunner to "gather" the missile after firing, so it is ineffective under 1,000 meters; but it makes up for this in a big way at 3,000 meters.

The big xenon searchlight is an anachronism on modern tanks, equipped with today's sophisticated passive night vision

devices, though still occasionally useful in the recon role. Back in the early 1970s it was commonly fitted; and, with use of a pink filter, this would extend the guidable range of the Shillelagh in marginal light conditions.

(Above) Looking from the loader's to the gunner's station, right of the unusual electrically powered breech of the 152mm gun/launcher. The early problems with the combustible case ammo have long been solved, partly by use of a "closed breech scavenger system" which blows compressed air violently through the tube after firing, scouring out any smouldering residue.

(Right) Gunner's station, looking forward and down; note elevation (left) and traverse controls.

Continued from page 106

and the evil reputation which clung to it after Vietnam. It was far better suited to the environment of Germany, however, where it served in numbers with US Army forces until the decision was taken to withdraw it in 1978.

One role for which the M551 remained uniquely suited, however, was to provide the paratroopers of the 82nd Airborne Division with air-droppable armor. The Sheridan can be delivered to the DZ either as a conventional heavy load by Low Velocity Air Drop (LVAD) under eight 100-foot parachutes; or - much more commonly - by Low Altitude Parachute Extraction (LAPSE), when a drogue chute drags the palletized tank out of the tail of a C-130 making a slow pass at very low altitude.

The division's integral tank battalion kept Sheridans right up into the 1990s, and they gave good service. The Sheridans of the 82nd's 3/73rd Armor were the first, and for weeks the only Coalition tanks facing Saddam Hussein across the Saudi Arabian border during Operation Desert Shield, arriving in August 1990. The only combat use of the Shillelagh missile came in Operation Desert Storm, when a round from a 3/73rd Sheridan demolished an Iraqi anti-tank gun bunker - as advertised....

Sheridans have recently been withdrawn from active service with the 82nd Airborne; but they still serve the US Army at the National Training Center, Fort Irwin, California - where you'll see M551s zipping around the desert battlefield in a variety of odd disguises. To boost the realism of their battle training, the Army modified some 300 M551s with fiberglass, sheet metal and wooden kits which mimic the basic appearance of Soviet AFVs - the T-72, BMP, 122mm SP howitzer, and ZSU-23-4 AA tank. Using the MILES computerised laser training system, these Opposing Forces provide a most effective "enemy" for US units rotating through Fort Irwin.

(Below) The right side of the turret interior, with gunner's (left) and TC's stations; the commander's seat is flipped up. Beneath the gunner's weapon selection instrumentation is the azimuth indicator allowing the M551 - like most modern US tanks before the Abrams - to provide very accurate indirect fire with HE rounds. Apart from his telescopic sight, for night work the gunner has an infrared M44 sight on the turret roof. The TC's controls are below and forward of his cupola - note all-round vision blocks.

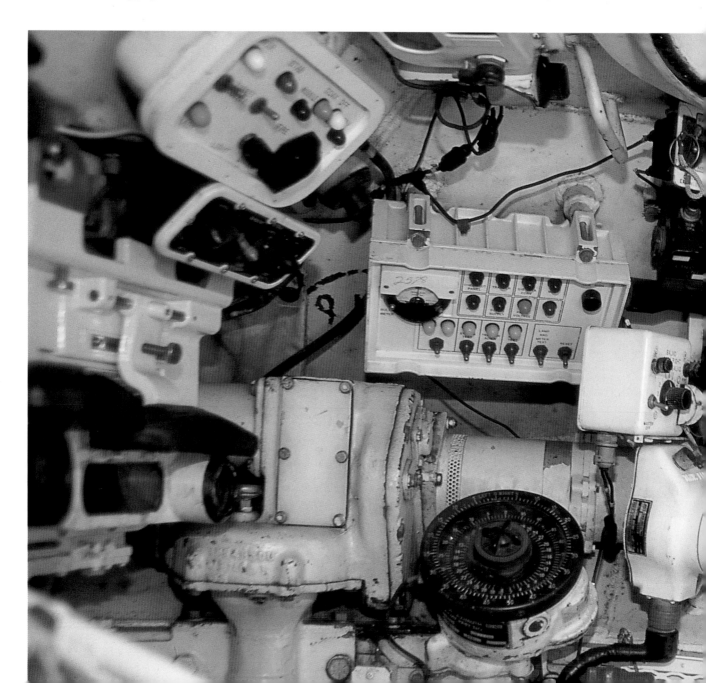

(**Right**) Commander's main gun override controls. The red palm switch on the right of the black grip energizes the electrical motors for the turret and gun, and disengages the gunner's control - as long as it is depressed, the TC has control of the gun. The white box ahead of it is the selector for the smoke grenade dischargers. On the turret wall at right are the commander's communications controls, above a first aid box.

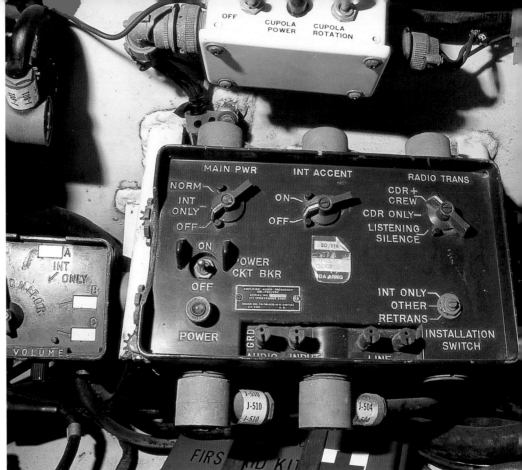

(Right) M551 commander's communications switchbox, below his cupola controls high on the right turret wall.

(Below) M551 main radio intallation, in the turret rear bustle behind and left of the commander's station.

Chapter 4
Desert Storm
T-72

Back in the mid-1970s, before anybody outside the Warsaw Pact got to play with one, the Soviet T-72 was a very fearsome beast. Intelligence reaching the West was incomplete and contradictory; guesswork about its unknown powers inflated it into a monster; but when NATO got further and better particulars, it became clear that though it was a very powerful, sleek, fast fighting machine, the T-72 had certainly not leapfrogged over current NATO designs.

Conversely, since hordes of Iraqi-crewed T-72s were easily demolished by Abrams and other more modern tanks during Operation Desert Storm in 1991, some commentators have tended to belittle it; and that's equally foolish, because it's an interesting, important example of the breed. Desert Storm did not, in fact, provide a fair comparison: the T-72 is the Russian equivalent of the American M60, not the Abrams. What's more, the models defeated so easily in Kuwait and Iraq were designed for export, with a lower specification than the Russian Army's tanks - and they were handled with striking incompetence by their unit commanders.

The T-72, like most weapons of Russian/Soviet design, is designed to be durable and efficient rather than fancy. It has thick, well-sloped armor, a huge gun and a powerful diesel engine. The sights are conventional, at least on the export versions, with low-light viewing capability but without the passive imaging system which distinguishes the latest Abrams, Challenger and Leopard. Its small turret, allowed by a two-man turret crew with mechanical loading, is the most immediately noticeable feature.

You don't really climb into the T-72 - you more or less put it on, like steel coveralls....If you drop down through the gunner's hatch on the left side of the turret, you find yourself encased in bits of machinery, weapons sights, and the auto-loading system for the gun on your right. It is a tight fit, unlike the Abrams and many other modern tanks. From the gunner's seat you can see very little except your sighting and viewing devices, about ten inches in front of your nose. The gunner's controls are very similar to those used by NATO tankers: a set of dual grip devices which can pivot back and forth to elevate and depress the huge 125mm "Rapier 3"

smoothbore gun, or rotate left or right to traverse the turret and gun. The gunner has control of a laser rangefinder, dual-axis stabilization system, co-axial machine gun, and infrared searchlight.

There is no loader in the T-72; the gun breech divides the little turret in two, with the gunner on the left and the TC on the right, and an automatic loading system below. Ammunition is stored in a 24-round carousel under the turret basket, the projectile and propellant components of the round stowed separately. The case is combustible except for a metal stub. During an engagement, the commander selects the type of ammunition needed (HE, HEAT, or APFSDS); the loading mechanism rotates the carousel, removes the right projectile and inserts it into the breech followed by the propellant, and the breech closes. The gunner fires; the gun recoils, and the stub endpiece is automatically extracted and ejected through a small port at the top rear of the turret. (This makes the T-72 doubly dangerous, as the US Army's Director of Combat Development found out while watching a demonstration from close up: the stub flew through the air, hit him on the head, and left the two-star general unconscious....)

Expert assessment

The Patton Museum at Fort Knox, Kentucky, owns several ex-Iraqi T-72s gathered up after Desert Storm in 1991, including at least one that is a double combat veteran - a neat line of 12.7mm bullet scars on the armor recalls some previous encounter with an Iranian unit during the "First Gulf War" of the 1980s. *Charles Lemons*, curator of the Patton Museum, has had the opportunity to drive the T-72 on many occasions; his report, in part, is as follows:

"There are some inherent problems with Soviet armored vehicles. One is that you've got to be sure to pressurize the hydraulic system before you shut down - or you don't have any brakes or clutch the next time you fire up. In that event, you'll jerk forward about five feet when the engine starts

because the clutch is engaged, whether you want it to be or not; and the brakes won't work until you get pressure. In fact, the clutch is either in or out - there's no feathering it gently to get started smoothly. The most important thing to remember is, at the end of the day, to push in the clutch, push in the brake, then reach down and lock them both - otherwise, the next time you start up you're going to kill somebody.

"Since the steering is also hydraulic, you loose authority when you push in the clutch - this really requires some adjustment on the part of the driver! You end up popping the clutch in and out and jerking the vehicle around more than you would do with a British or American tank. Unlike US tanks, the steering is also very jerky: you pull back on a lateral, and when the system engages, you turn - right now! At higher speeds there is a delay in steering release that seems designed into the system, and the higher the gear, the longer the delay. If you're cruising down the battlefield in 5th or 6th gear, the steering will smooth out, but you'll find that there's a noticeable delay before changes in steering to take effect - that also takes some getting used to. And the driver has to be buttoned up to fight the vehicle, unlike the Abrams and many other contemporary main battle tanks.

"Generally, the T-72 is pretty noisy, and extremely smoky (I can't believe how much smoke those things put out, even when new) - but they will run on just about anything.

"The T-72 is the Soviet equivalent of the US M60, not the M1 Abrams, despite all the comparisons made between the two. It has some deficiencies, and some virtues, for a main battle tank of the Cold War era. One problem is that the ammunition is mostly stowed in a carousel directly under the turret; all you have to do is get a round in between the road wheels, and you're pretty well guaranteed to have a secondary explosion that destroys the tank and instantly kills the crew.

"But the fire control system is excellent: it has a laser rangefinder that works quite well and a good fire control computer, and the infamous auto- loader actually works pretty well. The 72's gun stabilizer is the equivalent of the M60's - it will lock onto a target and track it; we've done it right here, and it works quite nicely. The TC's target desig-

(Opposite & above)
This T-72 was built in Czechoslovakia in 1983, and supplied to the East German Army; some Western sources term this model the T-72G. One characteristic, later replaced by conventional rigid skirt plates, was this set of spring-loaded "gill" armor panels, seen above fully deployed. Note, above left, the smoothbore muzzle of the 125mm Rapira 3 gun; and the active infrared searchlights slaved to the gun and the TC's cupola.

nator has the oddest set-up I have ever seen, though, with those handles sticking up.

"It has another odd feature, which is that the turret will wobble back and forth unless you've got the turret lock engaged, or power applied to the system. Otherwise the turret will swing back and forth a bit as the tank corners left and right, which is a bit disconcerting. Operating the turret lock is also a real pain compared to other tanks - it has to be hand-cranked into the locked position, and hand-cranked out again. That will slow you down in a combat situation, and you might not be able to get the lock off in time to save your life.

"The radio equipment is buried in the hull, along with everything else. A lot of the switches are hidden, and you have to learn where they are to get things to work, unlike in an M60, where everything is in plain view. Unless you know exactly what you're working with, it could get real confusing. But once you know where all the switches are it's kind of idiot-proof. The stabilization system is another example: it takes four switches to turn it on, and two of those are out of sight.

"Despite the tiny spaces and apparently cramped conditions, we worked with a guy who had been in the East German Army and was all of 6ft 2in tall - and he slid into the fighting compartment without any trouble at all, and seemed perfectly comfortable. He probably couldn't do that in the driver's compartment, though. The engine runs smoothly enough, and has plenty of power, but it isn't a comfortable tank to drive. If you're as tall as I am - 5ft 4in - you're too tall

(Left) Convoy station-keeping light on the rear of the turret.

(Right) The small T-72 turret from the left rear. The tank stands less than eight feet high, but the limited depression allowed by the gun's low mounting partly cancels out this advantage when in hull defilade positions. The gunner's hatch is at left, the commander's at right, and between them the ejection port for the used shell case stubs. Maximum armor protection for the turret is around 275mm in the forward quadrant (the glacis is about 200mm, the rest of the hull about 70mm maximum).

to read half of the gauges. The NBC controls and batteries are right next to you, boxing you in. It is possible to get out the escape hatch, and to squirm back through the turret if necessary, but both are extremely cramped; if you need to get out fast, you're probably dead.

"The auto-loader is supposed to be dangerous to the gunner, and you hear stories about gunners having their arms crushed in the thing; actually, in my experience, the tube - when controlled by the gun stabilization device - is more dangerous to the commander. With the gun depressed, the loader can potentially crush the arm of the TC against the turret roof if he doesn't keep out of the way. And when you're distracted by searching for targets and watching what's going on outside the tank, it's easy to get in range of the loader. That happened to me while trying to designate a target on the move, travelling about 30km/h over rough terrain; the stabilizer was keeping the gun level, and as the hull pitched up and down the gun swung up and down, with the breech tapping me on the elbow. Once I discovered what was bumping me I got my arm out of the way; if we had really pitched down and the breech pitched up any higher, I would likely have been injured.

"It's a robust vehicle, with moderately good speed - not as good as an M1, but equivalent to the M60; and that's what the T-72 is, really. Why did it do so badly in the Gulf War? For one thing, it was totally outclassed by the M1, a newer generation tank. It still uses 'active infrared' imaging, a sure way to become a target for any modern tank with thermal sights. Another problem was that the crews were totally inept and demoralized. And yet another factor was that the tanks that we captured from the Iraqis are the export version, not the top-of-the-line model."

(Right & below right)
Inside surfaces of the commander's and gunner's hatch covers; they are designed to stand upright and provide protection from small arms when the crewmen are standing in the hatches, and are locked in position by the small handles near the bottom edge. Note the textured surfaces: this is anti-spall lining, a sort of "lead foam" material added to the inner surfaces of most modern tank turrets and fighting compartments. It provides a degree of protection against the fragments from the inner surface of the armor which are often knocked off by the impact of an AP round which fails to penetrate.

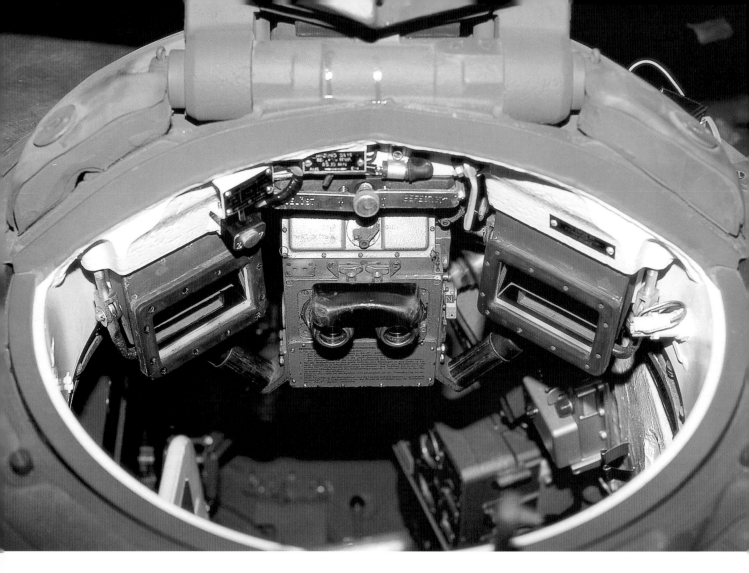
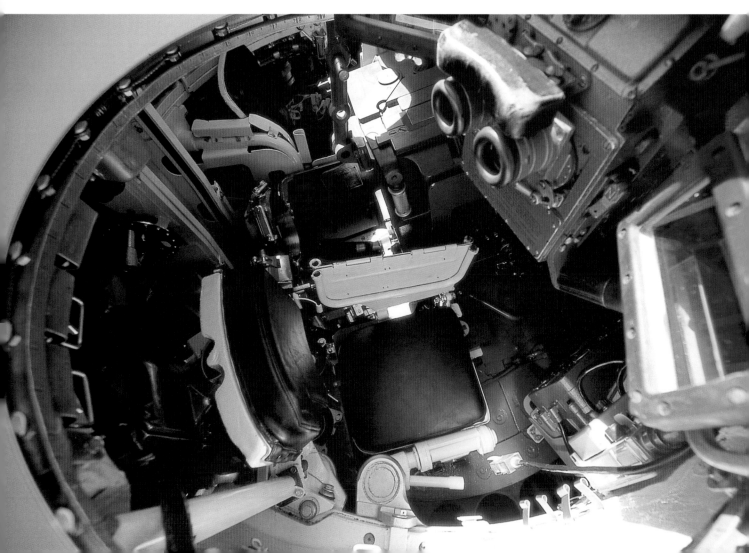

(Above left) The T-72 commander's station, looking down and forward from outside his hatch. Note vision blocks, gun sighting/target designation system and control handles - as in most modern tanks, the TC can override the gunner's controls and engage targets himself.

(Above) The commander's station, looking right across the breech from the gunner's station. The impression of space is a deceptive effect of the lens used to get this shot; this turret is a very tight fit, to Western eyes, and you certainly can't stretch out for a snooze. Crew comfort has never been a major factor in tank design.

(Left) The commander's station, looking down into the hatch at the seat, and left over the gun breech towards the gunner's station - the gun points to the right of this photo.

(Right) T-72 commander's controls, all within easy reach of his right hand on the wall of the turret below his hatch. Note propellor-shaped air circulation fan.

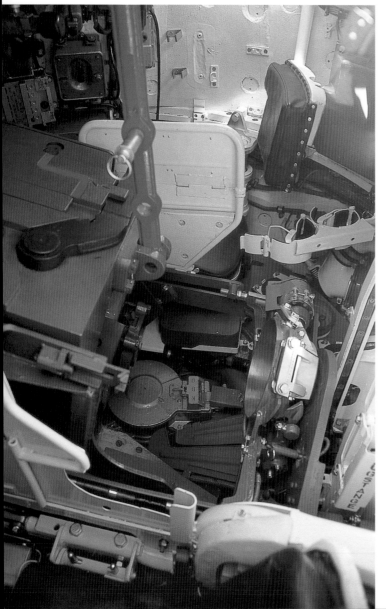

(Above) The T-72 gunner's controls and instrumentation on the left of the Rapira 3 gun; he has an efficient laser rangefinder and fire control computer, though the "active" infrared night vision system is dangerously outdated. His primary gun control grips are the red-brown plastic handles low at center right. Note the turret position indicator left of this. (Having served in the DDR, this tank's labelling is partly in Russian, partly in German.) The US Army rates the 125mm gun as effective to 2,000 meters, a little over a mile - considerably less than the 120mm round fired by the M1A1, rated effective to 3,000 meters.

(Left) Looking from the gunner's hatch to the right, across the breech to the commander's station - the gun points to the left in this photo. The red bar is a travel lock, keeping the gun rigid during non-tactical road marches. Behind the breech, part of the carousel of the controversial auto-loading system is clearly visible. Horror stories about the auto-loader biting bits off crewmen were rife some years ago; but the

problems dated from an immature version invented for the earlier T-64 tank (christened by its crews "The Steel Grave"), and it seems to work efficiently now - although rate of fire is much slower than for manually-loaded NATO tank guns. When the 24 rounds in the carousel are expended it has to be refilled manually from another 16 rounds stowed elsewhere in the hull - a slow and awkward process.

M1 Abrams

The M1 Abrams is one of the two or three most advanced tanks in the world today, and the most battle-proven of that handful. It excels in each of the fundamentals of armored warfare - firepower, protection and mobility. The M1A1 variant performed spectacularly well in Desert Storm, its 120mm gun and state-of-the-art fire control systems routinely killing enemy tanks at over three kilometers range, in conditions which left enemy tankers entirely blind to its presence. Its sophisticated composite armor threw off the few Iraqi anti-tank rounds that managed to find their targets. And the Abrams' once-derided 1,500 horsepower gas turbine engine propelled its 50-ton bulk fast and reliably across the desert under the very worst conditions.

Back at the start of the 1980s, when the program was in its early stages, it was criticised by politicians and journalists as being far too complicated to work, and too expensive to buy. Unburdened by any real knowledge of what they were talking about, they were confused by superficial parallels - the M551 Sheridan scandal, and the heavy losses of Israeli tanks to enemy infantry in the 1973 Yom Kippur War. In fact, the Abrams has proved not only a remarkable success story, but a step upward to a whole new level of tank performance - a level which (so far...) it occupies virtually alone.

The fighting compartment

Like most tanks, the normal way to mount it is at the front near the idler wheel. Stick the toe of your boot in the loop provided under the track skirt, find a handhold, and pull yourself up. The turret looks massive, but you can climb up to the loader's hatch from the left side. Inside, the turret is fairly roomy - especially after the T-72. To expand on the introductory tour on pages 9 to 11 of this book:

An immediately striking difference is the absence of visible stowed ammunition. The shells are stored in the turret bustle - 55 rounds for the 105mm gun in the M1, or 34 of the larger 120mm rounds in the M1A1, with 17 of them immediately accessible in a ready rack behind an armored door on the left side. (Veteran combat tankers would think these dangerously

M1 Abrams of the 4th Infantry Division's integral armored component, prowling the tactical training area around Fort Carson, Colorado. An M1 battalion has 58 tanks - four companies each of three platoons each of four tanks, plus HQ and specialist tanks. In battle each element works in concert with its pair - each tank supports a partner, and the platoon fights as two pairs of tanks, following classic fire-and-movement principles.

The boxy shape of turret and hull are governed by the space needed for the highly protective Chobham armor; details are still classified, but the armor incorporates spaced layers of steel plate and ceramic bars, to frustrate both kinetic-energy and chemical-energy AT ordnance. On the turret roof, left of the gun, the armored doors protecting the optics of the gunner's and commander's integrated day/night sights are open.

low stocks to take into a serious battle; but the much greater chance of first-shot kills makes them adequate.) The shielded-off rack is an important improvement in safety: if the turret is penetrated and the propellant in the stored ammo detonates, blow-off panels in the roof should channel the force of the explosion upwards and away from the fighting compartment - historically, a hot AP round through the ammo bins often killed the crew in a catastrophic explosion.

The Abrams loader has a seat in the rear left corner, to help protect him from being thrown around and injured when the tank is moving fast across country; he also has to watch out for the moving breech when the stabilized gun is tracking automatically. The tank's radio is installed to his left front, up beside the gun, along with MG ammunition and other stowage.

The gunner is conventionally stationed on the right of the main gun - the rifled 105mm M68A1 in the M1, and the big smoothbore 120mm M256 in the M1A1. Each takes two

Continued on page 124

(Left) Abrams at speed; its unique AGT-1500 gas turbine guzzles fuel - about 3.5gals per mile across country - but is smaller, lighter, and needs less maintenance than a comparable diesel. The M1 can track and engage targets while travelling across country at speeds of 30-40mph.

(Below & right) Gunner and TC in their stations, the commander searching the scenery through his vision blocks, right hand gripping his CPC override gun control stick - ahead of this is the CWS control. The white element just below the red cupola crank handle is the TC's .50cal machine gun sight; left of this is his main GPS Extension sight.

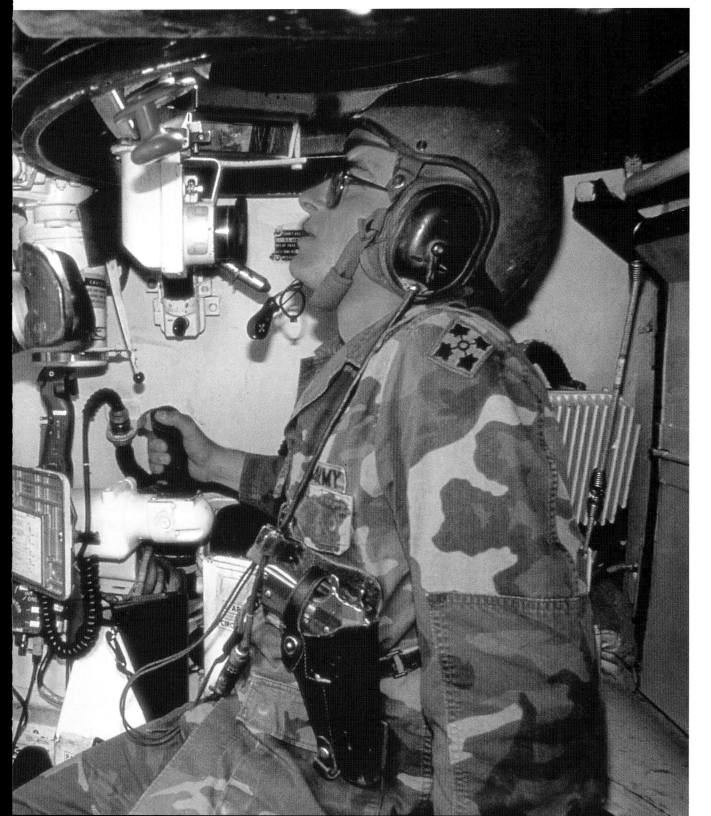

main types of ammunition: High Explosive Anti-Tank (HEAT), and Armor Piercing Fin Stabilized Discarding Sabot (APFSDS). The distinction between rifled and smoothbore guns is worth a brief explanation.

In simple terms, smoothbore guns (as preferred by the German, and lately the Russian and American armies) can take ammo giving a very high muzzle velocity, which suits the modern kinetic-energy penetrators used against enemy tanks - the APFSDS rounds - which fly far and fast on a rather flat trajectory for maximum accuracy. But because there is no rifling in the barrel to impart a twist and keep it stable, the projectile has to have built-in stabilizing fins. The trade-off is that the high explosive rounds needed to engage other types of target are less effective - the fin- stabilized HEAT rounds are measurably less useful against infantry, gunpits, etc. than the equivalent shells from rifled guns.

The first M1 Abrams, and the British Challenger, have respectively 105mm and 120mm rifled guns. These can still fire effective APFSDS ammo; but also High Explosive Squash Head (HESH) rounds, which do much more damage to a much wider range of targets. Smoothbore enthusiasts claim that non-armor targets are the business of the artillery, anyway; rifle devotees argue that you're better off with a wide range of unpleasantness in your racks, because you can't be sure the artillery will be around when you need them urgently. Everything is a trade-off, and both schools are right.

The gunner's job is battlefield surveillance, target acquisition, and engagement. During combat he sits leaning forward, wedged into the space between the seat and sights by head and chest pads to minimize the effect of the tank's motion on his sight picture. His GPS sighting system and fire control computer have enough switches and indicator lights for an aircraft cockpit - the procedure for set-up, tracking and engaging is described in the captions on page 127. In basic terms: his sights allow him to acquire a target under conditions and at ranges undreamt-of by previous generations of tank crews; and his computer keeps his aim true until he fires, calculating and collating many variables which earlier tankers had no way of even measuring, let alone factoring in.

The Abrams commander

The commander is kept busy ensuring that his tank is playing its assigned role in the larger scheme of the operation: peering out of the hatch, listening to radio traffic on the company net, scanning for targets, and keeping the rest of the crew from getting complacent.

His station allows for four observation positions, from standing waist-high in the open hatch (the best view, but the worst protection), to seated under a closed hatch (the worst view, with the best protection). He has six periscopes in his cupola; and his hatch can either be tipped open in the usual way, or raised about eight inches vertically and locked, giving an unobstructed view all round while protecting him from artillery air-bursts and other hazards from above.

The TC has a .50cal machine gun mounted on a ring round his cupola, and the loader can mount a 7.62mm MG on a pintle outside his hatch. In World War II the theory was that external MGs were useful against both ground attack aircraft and infantry and "soft-skin" targets, and co-axial and front hull MGs with limited movement could be used against the latter. Modern jets are too fast, and modern attack helicopters too well armored (and fire missiles from too long a range), for hand-aimed MGs to be any use today; but the threat of man-carried anti-tank weapons has grown steadily since World War II. The awesome .50cal/12.7mm MG remains accurate and deadly against any ground target unprotected by tank-grade armor, and if the TC can use it without lethally exposing himself to return fire it remains a worthwhile addition to the tank's armament. Co-axial guns can be tracked, aimed and fired accurately from inside the tank, and are still typically fitted; the old bow-mounted "bullet hoses" have been discarded, along with the "fifth man" position in the hull front.

In the Abrams the commander's .50cal can be fired remotely from under armor with the Commander's Weapon Station control. You power up the CWS, and remove the control handle from its bracket with your right hand. Depressing a palm switch gives you power to traverse the turret with a thumb button, left or right. Place your left hand on the elevation crank handle to the left of the sight for the .50cal; and aim by traversing with your right hand and the thumb button on the CWS, and elevating with the crank in your left hand. The safety is a sliding switch on the shaft of the CWS control; once you've lined up the target, switch from SAFE to FIRE, and gently pull the knob on the handle with your left hand - the .50cal will fire until you release it. Through the sight you watch bright red fireballs float rapidly downrange; one in every six rounds in the belt is a tracer.

As in most modern tanks, the Abrams commander has priority control of the main gun if he wants it; although he can't feed manual input into the ballistic computer panel from his station, his sight gives him the same automatically corrected picture as the gunner's, and he can aim and fire with as much precision. He operates the gun with a right hand grip, the Commander's Power Control. The TC selects the main gun on his control panel, and views the target through his sight (the Commander's GPS Extension). The palm switch on his handle energizes the turret and gun hydraulics, takes control away from the gunner, and allows the TC to aim the gun. A button on top of the control handle "lases" the target to measure the range, which feeds directly into the ballistic computer; then a trigger button under the right index finger fires the gun.

M1 Abrams Road Report

The driving position is unusual; the driver lies almost prone on his back in a comfortable seat. This, and his hand controls, can be raised or lowered for "head out" or "buttoned up" driving positions. He drives holding something resembling a small pair of motorbike handle-bars, with twist-grip controls. He has a passive night vision device; in the latest variant he may also have a thermal sight, but in its absence he can still be guided by instructions from the TC using one.

Duane Klug: "The Abrams is extremely responsive, particularly considering its bulk, with great acceleration and very responsive brakes - I gave my driving instructor bruises from my first couple of stops in the Abrams. It steers easily and naturally."

(Above left & above) The loader, dressed in wood-land-camo BDUs and CVC helmet, gets the order from the commander to select High Explosive Anti-Tank (note the intercom switch-box behind his right shoulder). He bangs the button for the ammo rack blast door with his right knee, and as it slides open he punches the base of the round he wants - he has previously marked "S" or "H" on the ends, for Sabot or HE. That springs the case a couple of inches out of the rack, so he can get his gloved fingers under the rim to pull it all the way out. The 105mm combat munitions have aluminum-color cases and black heads - this one, the squared-off end with protruding electric detona-tor which identifies the shaped-charge, chemical-energy HEAT round. (All inert training rounds are painted bright blue.) The black levers at turret ring level are traverse locks.

(Above & right) He extracts the round; in a combat situation he would hit the knee button again to close the blast doors immediately. He flips the heavy shell end for end while he pivots to his left, aligning it with the M68A1 gun breech. He feeds it in with his left hand, then shoves it home with his closed right fist. (Some tankers are taught to shove with the heel of the open hand, fingers extended upwards; it doesn't much matter, as long as the fingers can't get amputated when the breech closes - which it does, automatically, as soon as the extractors are tripped.) Then he pushes the safety control to FIRE, and shouts "Up!" to let the gunner know the round is ready to go. A loader should be able to keep the gun fed fast enough to sustain a rate of fire of ten to twelve rounds per minute - one every five or six seconds.

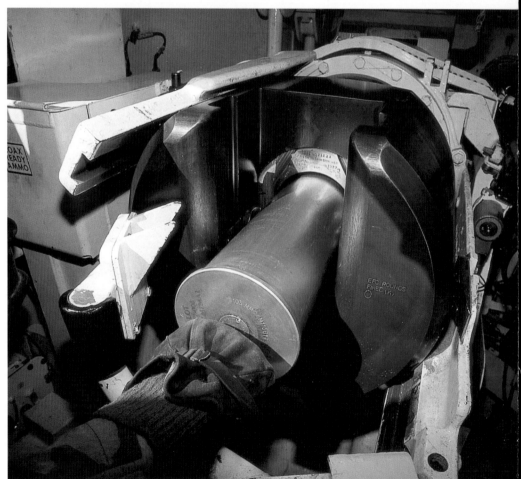

The M1 gunner's station - **(right)** unoccupied but lit up, and **(below)** with a trooper in the saddle. Above the black "Cadillacs" - the handles of the gunner's traverse, elevation, laser rangefinder and firing controls - are the headrest for the Gunner's Primary Sight (GPS) system; and his gun control switches and lights - main gun or co-ax selector, ammunition type selector, optical or thermal imaging selector, sight magnification, sight polarity and contrast, reticle symbology....

To his right is the fire control computer - on the closed cover this gunner has scrawled a tally of number and type of rounds fired recently. The gunner manually inputs data on air temperature, barometric pressure, and ammo type; but the computer automatically gathers data from sensors on the tilt angle of the tank, the crosswind velocity, and gun tube warp.

He acquires the target in his sights, bringing the gun to bear using the standard G-shaped approach, and "lases" it with the rangefinder button on his controls; the range is calculated almost instantaneously. If the target is moving, he tracks it with his controls - the stabilization system makes this fairly easy, with practice; the computer collates all the deflection factors, and simply off-sets the reticle in the gunner's sights. Even when moving across country, with his target also moving at some oblique angle, all he has to do is maintain a good sight picture until he squeezes the trigger button.

0890

(Above) At first sight this eerie green picture resembles that of a standard image intensification night sight, which works by gathering and enhancing natural moonlight and starlight. But this image is provided by an M1's thermal sights; it doesn't use light, it uses the tell-tale heat of these two tanks - and even through a dense chemical smokescreen they would still be sitting ducks. The sight reticle is aligned dead on the right hand target's center-of-mass, as per the manual....In Kuwait and Iraq the thermal sight allowed Abrams crews to engage on the darkest night or in the worst daytime conditions - with their conventional optics blinded by oily black smoke, or flying dust, which is often kicked up in huge and persistent clouds in front of a tank by the gun's muzzle blast.

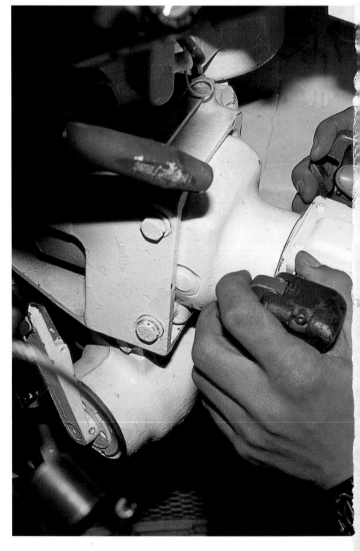

(Right) The moment of truth. If the trigger on the Cadillacs fails - as it has done for the author - then the red handle just above the gunner's left hand is the emergency firing device or "blaster", a small electric generator which will unfailingly put fire in the hole.